American Red Cross

America's Relief Expedition to Asia Minor under the Red Cross

American Red Cross

America's Relief Expedition to Asia Minor under the Red Cross

ISBN/EAN: 9783337248840

Printed in Europe, USA, Canada, Australia, Japan

Cover: Foto ©ninafisch / pixelio.de

More available books at **www.hansebooks.com**

RED CROSS HEADQUARTERS, CONSTANTINOPLE.

REPORT

AMERICA'S RELIEF EXPEDITION

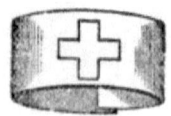

TO ASIA MINOR

UNDER THE RED CROSS

WASHINGTON, D. C.

1896

PRINTED BY
THE JOURNAL PUBLISHING COMPANY,
MERIDEN, CONN.

REPORT OF

MISS CLARA BARTON,

PRESIDENT AND TREASURER OF THE AMERICAN

NATIONAL RED CROSS.

To the People of the United States:

IN November, 1895, while busily occupied in editing a history of the Red Cross for publication, the press commenced to warn us of a possible call for the relief of the terrible sufferings of Armenia, which were engaging the attention of the civilized world. These warnings were followed later by a letter from Rev. Judson Smith, D. D., of Boston, Secretary of the American Board of Commissioners for Foreign Missions referring his suggestion back to Rev. Henry O. Dwight, D. D., of the American Board of Foreign Missions at Constantinople. The American Red Cross was requested by these representative gentlemen, to undertake the distribution of relief funds among the sufferers of Armenia. Owing to the disturbed condition of the country and of its strict laws, combined as they were with existing racial and religious differences, it was found almost impossible at the moment to distribute the relief needed. The faithful but distressed resident missionaries were themselves helpless sufferers to a great extent and practically prisoners in their own houses. These had not always been spared to them in the wild excitement which reigned for several months previous, otherwise they would have been the normal channels for distributing aid. This written request from Dr. Smith was nearly identical with a similar one from Mr. Spencer Trask, of New York, who, with others, was about to form a National Armenian Relief Committee, to be established in that city. Following their letters, both of these gentlemen, Dr. Smith and Mr. Trask, came to Washington to personally urge our compliance with the request that we accept the charge of this distribution of relief funds. Accustomed to the trials, responsibilities and hardships of field relief labor, this proposition seemed something to be shrunk from rather than accepted and we naturally hesitated. The idea, however, became public, and a general importunity on the part of the people became prevalent. The necessity for immediate action was urged; human beings were starving and could not be reached, hundreds of towns and villages had not been heard from since the fire and sword went over them, and no one else was so well prepared for the work of field relief, it was said, as ourselves. It was urged that we had a trained force of field workers, and as Turkey was one of the signatory powers to the Red Cross treaty of Geneva, having given its adhesion as long ago as July, 1865, it must consequently be familiar with its methods and humanitarian ideas. Thus it was hoped that she would the more readily accept its presence than that of a more strange body of workers. These are only a shadowing of the reasons urged on behalf of our acceptance. Under this pressure, coupled with our strong sympathies, the subject was taken into serious consideration with the simple demand on our part of two positive assurances: First, we must be assured by the committees that we were the choice of the people of the entire country, that there was no opposition to us, and that there was perfect unanimity between themselves; there must be nowhere any discord; the task would be difficult enough under the best conditions. Second, that they had the funds to distribute. Assured on both these points, our promise was given that we would go and do our best to make the desired distribution in the interior of Asia Minor.

With this ray of hope that something might be done, the pent-up sympathies of the people burst forth. Public meetings were held, addresses made, Armenian conditions estimated, horrors reproduced, responsibilities placed, causes canvassed, and opinions expressed; honest, humane, and entirely natural, precisely the course to rouse public sentiment and indignation, if that were the only or the main object in view. In consideration, however, of the relief effort, it was of questionable wisdom perhaps, when it is borne in mind that we had yet to ask the opening of a door hitherto closed against the world, when we needed permission to enter, in order to reach the starving sufferers with the relief that was planning for them. In the enthusiasm of the hour, this fact seemed to be entirely lost sight of. It also seemed to be forgotten that if this difficult and delicate task were to be assigned to the Red Cross and its officers, that the making of their mission or of themselves personally, prominent or laudatory features of public gatherings where Ottoman officials or representatives were always listeners, could not fail to render the post more difficult, and prospects of success more doubtful.

The international and neutral character of the Red Cross, as a medium of relief in mitigation of war or overwhelming calamity, appeared to be overlooked or wholly misunderstood. It was not recognized that only by abstaining from discordant opinions could we be in a position to perform our work. By the obligations of the Geneva treaty, all national controversies, racial distinctions, and differences in creed must be held in abeyance and only the needs of humanity considered. In this spirit alone can the Red Cross meet its obligations as the representative of the nations and governments of the world acting under it. But American enthusiasm is boundless, and its expression limitless; and the same breath that crushed the Ottoman Empire, scattered it to the winds or sunk it in the lowest depths, elevated the Red Cross and its proposed relief out of sight among the clouds. Precautionary remonstrance from us was in vain, but it was not until after we had publicly given our consent, made all arrangements and appointed our aids, that the fruits of these ardent demonstrations became visible in a pronunciamento through the Turkish Minister resident at Washington, prohibiting the Red Cross from entering Turkey.

I found this decision on the part of the Bey and his government very natural and politically justifiable — our own government and people would probably have done the same or even more under similar conditions, provided similar conditions could have existed among them. I was ready to abide by the decision and remain at home. This, neither people nor committees, would consent to. Of course our selected force of more than a score of trained and experienced field workers, each a specialist, must be given up. If any relief were now attempted it could only be individual, with two or three officers from headquarters as indispensable aids.

Previous to the announcement of the Turkish Minister prohibiting the Red Cross from entering Turkey, the promise had been gained from us to leave by the S. S. "New York" on the 22d of January, and notwithstanding the reply to a cablegram from the Department of State to Constantinople, asking if the prohibition against the entrance of the Red Cross was really official and from the government itself, or but semi-official, had not been received, our promise was kept and we sailed with this uncertainty resting over us.

The picture of that scene is still vivid in my memory. Crowded piers, wild with hurrahs, white with parting salutes, hearts beating with exultation and expectation—a little shorn band of five, prohibited, unsustained either by government or other authority, destined to a port five thousand miles away, from approach to which even the powers of the world had shrunk. What was it expected to do or how to do it? Visions of Don Quixote and his windmills loomed up, as I turned away and wondered.

A week at sea, to be met at midnight at Southampton, by messenger down from London, to say that the prohibition was sustained, the Red Cross was forbidden, but that such persons as our Minister, Mr. Terrell, would appoint, would be received. Here was another delicate uncertainty which could not be committed to Ottoman telegraph, and Dr. Hubbell was dispatched alone to Constantinople (while we waited in London) to learn from Mr. Terrell his attitude toward ourselves and our mission. Under favorable responses we proceeded, and reached Constantinople on February 15th; met a most cordial reception from all our own government officials, and located *pro tem* at Pera Palace Hotel; it being so recently after the Stamboul massacres that no less public place was deemed safe.

The following day we received in a body the members of the Missionary Board in Constantinople, including its treasurer, W. W. Peet, Esq., and Dr. Washburn, president of Robert College, and here commenced that friendly intercourse which continued without interruption, strengthening as the days wore on through the half year that followed, till moistened eyes and warm hand grasp at parting told more plainly than words how fraught with confidence that intercourse had been. If one would look for peers of this accomplished Christian body of our countrymen, they would only be found in the noble band of women, who, as wives, mothers and teachers, aid their labors and share their hardships, privations and dangers. I shall always feel it a privilege and an honor to have been called, even in a small way, to assist the efforts of this chosen body of our countrymen and women, whose faithful and devoted lives are made sacred to the service of God and their fellow men.

The first step was to procure an introduction to the Government which had in one sense refused me; and accompanied by Minister Terrell and his premier interpreter, Gargiulo, perhaps the longest serving and one of the most experienced diplomatic officers in Constantinople, I called by appointment upon Tewfik Pasha, the Turkish Minister of Foreign affairs or Minister of State. To those conversant with the personages connected with Turkish affairs, I need not say that Tewfik Pasha is probably the foremost man of the Government; a manly man, with a kind, fine face, and genial, polished manners. Educated abroad, with advanced views on general subjects, he impresses one as a man who would sanction no wrong it was in his power to avert.

We were received at the Department of State in an uninterrupted interview lasting over an hour. As this was the main interview and the base of all our work, it is perhaps proper that I give it somewhat in detail. Mr. Terrell's introduction was most appropriate and well expressed, bearing with strong emphasis upon the suffering condition of the people of the interior in consequence of the massacres, and the great sympathy of the people of America, their intense desire to help them, the heartfelt interest in their missionaries whose burdens were greater than they ought to bear, and the desire to aid them, and that for all these reasons we had been asked to come; that our objects were purely humanitarian, having neither political, racial, or religious bearing as such; that as the head of the organization thus represented I *could* have no other ideas, and it was the privilege of putting these ideas into practice and the protection required meanwhile that the people of America, through him and through me, were asking.

The Pasha listened most attentively to the speech of Mr. Terrell, thanked him, and replied that this was well understood; that they knew the Red Cross and its president, and turning to me repeated: "We know you, Miss Barton; have long known you and your work. We would like to hear your plans for relief and what you desire."

I proceeded to state them, bearing fully upon the fact that the condition to which the people of the interior of Asia Minor had been reduced by recent events had aroused the sympathy of the entire American people until they asked, almost to the extent of a demand, that assistance from them should be allowed to go directly to these sufferers, hundreds of whom had friends and relatives in America—a fact which naturally strengthened both the interest and the demand; that it was at the request of our people, *en masse*, that I and a few assistants had come; that our object would be to use the funds ourselves among the people needing them wherever they were found, in helping them to resume their former positions and avocations, thus relieving them from continued distress, the State from the burden of providing for them, and other nations and people from a torrent of sympathy which was both hard to endure and unwholesome in its effects; that I had brought skilled agents, practical and experienced farmers whose first efforts would be to get the people back to their deserted fields and provide them with farming implements and material wherewith to put in summer crops and thus enable them to feed themselves. These would embrace plows, hoes, spades, seed-corn, wheat, and later, sickles, scythes, etc., for harvesting, with which to save the miles of autumn grain which we had heard of as growing on the great plains already in the ground before the trouble; also to provide for them such cattle and other animals as it would be possible to purchase or to get back; that if some such thing were not done before another winter, unless we had been greatly misinformed, the suffering there would shock the entire civilized world. None of us knew from personal observations, as yet, the full need of assistance, but had reason to believe it very great. That if my agents were permitted to go, such need as they found they would be prompt to relieve. On the other hand, if they did not find the need existing there, none would leave the field so gladly as they. There would be no respecting of persons; humanity alone would be their guide. "We have," I added, "brought only ourselves, no correspondent has accompanied us, and we shall have none, and shall not go home to write a book on Turkey. We are not here for that. Nothing shall be done in any concealed manner. All dispatches which we send will go openly through your own telegraph, and I should be glad if all that we shall write could be seen by your Government. I cannot, of course, say what its character will be, but can vouch for its truth, fairness and integrity, and for the conduct of every leading man who shall be sent. I shall never counsel nor permit a sly or underhand action with your Government, and you will pardon me, Pasha, if I say that I shall expect the same treatment in return—such as I give I shall expect to receive."

Almost without a breath he replied—"And you shall have it. We honor your position and your wishes will be respected. Such aid and protection as we are able to, we shall render."

I then asked if it were necessary for me to see other officials. "No," he replied, "I speak for my Government;" and with cordial good wishes, our interview closed.

I never spoke personally with this gentleman again; all further business being officially transacted through the officers of our Legation. Yet I can truly say, as I have said of my first meeting with our matchless band of missionary workers, that here commenced an acquaintance which proved invaluable, and here were given pledges of mutual faith of which not a word was ever broken or invalidated on either side, and to which I owe what we were able to do through all Asia Minor. It is to the strong escorts ordered from the Sublime Porte for our expeditions and men, that I owe the fact that they all came back to me, and that I bring them home to you, tired and worn, but saved and useful still.

Dr. Hubbell, and the leaders of the five expeditions tell us that they were never, even for a portion of a day without an escort for protection, and this at the expense of the Turkish Government, and that without this protection they must not and could not have proceeded.

This interview with Tewfik Pasha was equal to a permit. Both Minister Terrell and myself cabled it to America as such. Dr. Hubbell, as general field agent, commenced at once to fit himself for a passage by the Black Sea, through Sivas to Harpoot. He had engaged a dragoman and assistants, and with Ernest Mason, who went with us as Oriental linguist, was prepared to ship next day, when at Sélamlik I was officially waited upon by a Court Chamberlain who informed me that although greatly regretting it, they were compelled to ask me to delay my expedition, in order to give the Government time to translate and read some of the immense quantities of newspaper matter which was being thrown in upon them from America, and which from its context appeared to be official, representing all our State Governors as engaged in a general move against Turkey, and that the chief seat of operations was the National Capitol. The Chamberlain tried by motions to show me that there were bushels of papers, and that it was impossible for them to translate them at once; that if they proved to be official as appeared by the great names connected with them, it was imperative that the Government consider them; but if it proved to be mere newspaper talk it was of no consequence, and I was begged to delay until they could investigate. Having received some specimens myself, I did not wonder at this request, I only wondered at the kindly courtesy with which it was made. I will take the liberty of inserting one of the clippings which I had received as a sample of what Turkey had to consider. This is only one among scores, which had led me to consider how, with these representations, we were ever to get any further:

PRO ARMENIAN ALLIANCE.

ITS WORK TO BE EXTENDED TO THE REMOTEST SECTIONS OF THE UNITED STATES. GOVERNORS OF STATES WILL AID.

[Special dispatch to the Sunday *Herald.*]

WASHINGTON, D. C., FEBRUARY 8, 1896.—The pro Armenian Alliance, with headquarters in this city, says the *Evening News*, which is working hand in glove with Miss Clara Barton and the Red Cross society for the relief of the Armenians, is rapidly completing arrangements for extending its work to the remotest sections of the United States. The permanent organization of the alliance was perfected in this city a little over a week ago, when the following officers were elected: President, R. S. Tharin; Vice-Presidents, B. Sunderland, D. D., and I. E. Gilbert, D. D.; Secretary, H. L. Sargent; Treasurer, F. A. Stier.

Within a few days the broadest promulgation of a pamphlet prepared by the alliance will begin.

On the title page of the little book will appear these unique mottos, "God against Allah, Christ against Mohammed, Bible against Koran, Heaven against Hell!"

It is proposed to proceed at once with the organization of local alliances throughout the Union, any person connected with a Christian organization or society, regardless of denomination, being eligible to membership.

* * * * * * * * * *

The headquarters of the alliance at the National Hotel are open from 10 to 12 o'clock.

It is intended to send out about 2,000,000 of the pamphlets explaining the purposes of the alliance, in lots of 200,000 or more. The delegates to the national convention will be selected by the different local clubs.

Well knowing, however, that investigation would show no trace of government or other official authority, we decided to lose no time, but to prepare ourselves for work at the earliest moment; and taking up the role of merchants, went into Stamboul, and purchased from the great wholesale houses, immense quantities of such material as could not fail of being useful and needed, to be later taken by caravan into the interior.

Just at this interval, a request was brought to me by Dr. Washburn, of Robert College, from Sir Philip Currie, English Ambassador, asking if I could not be "persuaded" to turn my expedition through the Mediterranean, rather than the Black Sea, in order to reach Marash and Zeitoun, where the foreign consuls were at the moment convened. They had gotten word to him that ten thousand people in those two cities were down with four distinct epidemics—typhoid and typhus fevers, disentery and small pox—that the victims were dying in overwhelming numbers and that there was not a physician among them, all being either sick or dead, with no medicines and little food. This was not a case for "persuasion," but of heartfelt thanks from us all that Sir Philip had remembered to call us whom he had never met. But here was a hindrance. The only means of conveyance from Constantinople to Alexandretta were coasting boats, belonging to different nationalities, and which left only once in two weeks and irregularly at that. Transport for our goods was secured on the first boat to leave, the goods taken to the wharf at Galata, and at the latest moment in order to give time, a request was made to the Government for *teskeres* or traveling permits for Dr. Hubbell and assistants. To our surprise they were granted instantly, but by some delay on the part of the messenger sent for them, they reached a moment too late; the boat left a little more than promptly, taking with it our relief goods, and leaving the men on the dock to receive their permits only when the boat was beyond recall. It was really the fault of no one. With the least possible delay the doctor secured passage by the first boat to Smyrna, and a fortunate chance boat from there, took him to Alexandretta, *via* Beyrout and Tripoli, Syria. The goods arrived in safety and two other of our assistants, whom we had called by cable from America, Messrs. Edward M. Wistar and Charles King Wood, were also passed over to the same point with more goods. There caravans were fitted out to leave over the, to them, unknown track to Aintab, as a first base. From this point the reports of each of these gentlemen made to me and compiled with this, will be living witnesses. I leave them to tell their own modest tales of exposure, severe travel, hard work and hardship, of which no word of complaint has ever passed their lips. There has been only gratitude and joy that they could do something in a cause at once so great and so terrible.

These little changes and accidents of travel, of not the slightest importance or concern to any one but ourselves, were naturally picked up and cabled to America as "news." The naming of the mere facts with neither explanations nor reasons assigned, could not be understood and only created confusion in the minds of the readers. They must, nevertheless, be accepted by our reporters, circulated, and discussed by our anxious people and perplexed committees.

The transcript of a paragraph from a letter received from America March 25, will serve to recall, at this late date, something of the state of feeling at the moment prevailing in America:

"Great doubt and dissatisfaction is felt here at the changeable course you seem to pursue—why you should propose to go first to the Black Sea, then to the Mediterranean, then not at all. Why to Smyna, then to Alexandretta, points where nothing is the matter and no help needed. They feel that you do not understand your own course, or are being deceived—will never get into the country—a fact which, it is said, is clearly seen here."

To further elucidate the intense feeling in our sympathetic country, we give a few sentences from other letters received at that time:

"What are those folks doing over there? First we hear they are going to Harpoot by the Black Sea, next they have gone to Smyrna, there is nothing the matter at Smyrna, next to Alexandretta; what have they gone there for? that is no place to go, any one can go to Alexandretta." "They don't seem to know what they *are* about." "They will never get into the country, we said so when they went, they ought to have known better themselves, we knew the Sultan would forbid them as he has; they are only being duped."

Unpleasant and somewhat ludicrous as these criticisms were, they served a purpose in coming back to us, as by them we were able to understand more fully the cables which had preceded them. "Give us news in full of your doings, it is important that we know." Every cable was answered with all the news we could send by that costly method.

I had asked permission and escort for two caravans from Alexandretta but had learned later from them that they would unite and go together to Aintab, in company with the Rev. Dr. Fuller of that city, who requires no introduction to the missionary or religious world. At this junction Mr. Gargiulo of the legation came to me in great haste (he having been sent for by the Sublime Porte), to know where our expeditions were. They had provided for two and could only get trace of one; where was the other? Please get definite information and let them know at once. I had served on too many battle fields not to understand what this meant. I knew our men were in danger somewhere, and some one was trying to protect them, and sent back the fullest information that there was but one expedition out, and waited. Two days later came the news of the massacre at Killis by the Circassians. Killis lay directly in their track, unknown to them, and the Turkish troops had unexpectedly come up and taken them on. I can perhaps, at this distant date, give no more correct note of this and the condition of things as found, than by an extract from a letter written by me at the time to our world's friend and mine, Frances Willard. We were at this moment securing the medical expedition for Marash and Zeitoun.

DEAR FRANCES WILLARD: * * * * * May I also send a message by you to our people, to your people and my people; in the name of your God and my God, ask them not to be discouraged in the good work they have undertaken. My heart would grow faint and words fail, were I to attempt to tell them the woes and the needs of these Christian martyrs. But what need to tell? They already know what words can say—alone, bereft, forsaken, sick and heartbroken, without food, raiment or shelter, on the snow-piled mountain sides and along the smoking valleys they wander and linger and perish. What more should I say to our people, but to show them the picture of what they themselves have already done.

The scores of holy men and women sustained by them, with prayers in their hearts, tears in their voices, hovering like angels and toiling like slaves, along all these borders of misery and woe, counting peril as gain and death as naught, so it is in His Name. But here another picture rises; as if common woe were not enough, the angel of disease flaps his black wings like a pall and in once bright Zeitoun and Marash contagion reigns. By scores, by hundreds, they die; no help, no medicine, no skill, little food, and the last yard of cotton gone to cover the sick and dying. To whom came the cry, "Help or we perish! Send us physicians!" The contributed gifts of America open the doors of classic Beyrout, and Ira Harris, with his band of doctors speeds his way. In Eskandaroon sleep the waiting caravans. The order comes, "Arise and go! henceforth your way is clear." Camels heavy laden, not with ivory and jewels, gold in the ingot and silk in the bales, but food and raiment for the starving, the sick, and the dying. Onward they sweep toward dread Killis—the wild tribe's knives before, the Moslem troops behind—"go on! we protect;" till at length the spires of Aintab rise in view. Weary the camels and weary the men — Hubbell, Fuller, Wistar, Wood, Mason—names that should live in story for the brave deeds of that march but just begun. The quick, glad cry of welcome of a city that had known but terror, sorrow and neglect for months—a little rest, help given, and over the mountains deep in snow, weary and worn their caravans go, toiling on towards fever and death. Let us leave them to their task. This is the work of America's people abroad. My message, through you, to her people at home—not to her small and poor, but to her rich and powerful people is, remember this picture and be not weary in well doing. CLARA BARTON.

While the first and second expeditions were fitting out from Alexandretta, the terrible state of things at Zeitoun and Marash was confirmed by the leading missionaries there, and we were asked to assume the expense of physicians, druggists, medicines and medical relief in general. This we were only too glad to do. Negotiations had already been opened by them with Dr. George E. Post of Beyrout, the glorious outcome of which was the going out of Dr. Ira Harris of Tripoli, Syria, with his corps of local physicians, and the marvelous results achieved. For some cause the doctor took the route via Adana, rather than by Alexandretta, and found himself in the midst of an unsafe country with insufficient escort. After a delay of two or three days, he got a dispatch to us at Constantinople. This dispatch was immediately sent through our Legation to the Porte, and directly returned to me with the written assurance that the proper steps had been instantly taken. On the same day Dr. Harris left Adana with a military escort that took his expedition through, leaving it only when safe in Marash.

Dr. Hubbell had arrived some days previous, but following instructions left immediately on the arrival of Dr. Harris, to pursue his investigations in the villages, and supply the general need of the people wherever found. This formed really the fourth expedition in the field at that early date, as the separate charges later so efficiently assumed by Messrs. Wistar and Wood, who were on the ground previous to the medical expedition, became known as the second and third expeditions.

It will be inferred that the assignment, furnishing and direction of these several expeditions, nearly a thousand miles distant, four weeks by personal travel, six weeks to write a letter and get reply, from two days to almost any time by telegraph, according to the condition of the wires, and in any language from Turkish and Greek to Arabic, with all other duties immediately surrounding, could not leave large leisure for home correspondence. While conscious of a restlessness on this score, we began to be mystified by the nature and text of dispatches from committees at home: "Contributors object to Turkish distribution." What could it mean? We could only reply: "Do not understand your dispatch. Please explain." These were followed by others of a similar character from other sources; finally letters, expressing great regret at the means to which I had been compelled to resort in order to accomplish my distribution, and the disastrous effect it could not fail to have upon the raising of funds. "Well, it was probably the only way to do, they had expected it, in fact, foretold it all the time."— What had I done? The mystery deepened. Finally, through the waste of waters and the lapse of time it got to me.—A little four line cablegram from Constantinople as follows:

"The council of ministers has decided that Miss Clara Barton can work only in conjunction with the Turkish commission in the distribution of relief, and can only use their lists of destitute Armenians. An Irade to that effect is expected."

No one had thought to inquire if this statement were *true*, no one had referred it to me, and as well as I ought to be known by our people, the question if I would be *likely* to take such a step, seems not to have been raised. It had been taken for granted through all America, England, and even the Missionary Boards of Turkey, that I had pledged myself and signed papers, to distribute the funds entrusted to me, under Turkish inspection and from lists furnished by Turkish officials. Myself and my officers appeared to be the only persons who had never heard of it. Astonished and pained beyond measure it was plainly and emphatically denied. Our press books of that date are marvels of denial. Sir Philip Currie and the Turkish Government itself, came to the rescue, declaring that no such course was ever intended. Secretary Olney was cabled to try "to make the people of America understand that the Turkish Government did not interfere with their distribution." In spite of all this, it went on until people and committees were discouraged; the latter cabling that in the present state of feeling little or nothing more could be expected, and gently suggesting the propriety of sending the balance in hand to other parties for distribution. My own National Red Cross officers in America, hurt and disgusted at the unjust form affairs were taking, in sympathy advised the leaving of the field and returning home.

Here was a singular condition of affairs. A great international work of relief, every department of which was succeeding beyond all expectation, wherein no mistakes had been made, letters of gratitude and blessing pouring in from every field of labor, finances carefully handled and no pressure for funds. On the other hand a whole nation in a panic, strong committees going to pieces, and brave faithful officers driven through pity to despair and contempt, and the cause about to be abandoned and given up to the lasting harm of all humanity. So desperate a case called for quick and heroic measures. Realizing the position of the committees from their own sad reports, I at once cabled relieving them from further contributions: "*We will finish the field without further aid.*" To my Red Cross officers I dictated the following letter, which I believe was used somewhat by the harrassed committees in struggling on to their feet again:

AYAZ-PACHA, TAXIM, CONSTANTINOPLE, April 18, 1896.
P. V. DeGraw, Esq., Corresponding Secretary,
American National Red Cross, Washington, D. C., U. S. A.

DEAR MR. DEGRAW: I received both your and Stephen E. Barton's heavy-hearted and friendly letters, and they fell on soil about as heavy. I could not understand how it could be, for I knew we had done our best and I *believed* the best that could have been done under the circumstances and conditions. I knew we held a great, well organized relief that would be needed as nothing else could be. That besides us, there was no one to handle the terrible scourge that was settling down—no one here, no one to come, who could touch it. I knew I was *not* interfered with; that no "restrictions" nor propositions had been imposed or even offered; that the Government was considerate and accorded all I asked. But what had stirred America up and set it, apparently, against us? The relief societies going to pieces, and turning sad glances here? We could not understand it. I did not wonder that you thought we "had best come home," still I knew we would not; indeed, we could not. I have a body of relief on these fields, hundreds of miles away in the mountains, a thousand miles from me, that I could not draw off in six weeks, and if we were to, it would be to abandon thousands of poor, sick, suffering wretches to a fate that ought to shock the entire world. Sick, foodless, naked, and not one doctor and no medicine among them; whole cities scourged and left to their fate, to die without a hand raised to help excepting the three or four resolute missionaries, tired, worn, God-serving, at their posts until they drop. The civilized world running over with skillful physicians, and not one there; no one to arrange to get them there; to pay expenses, take special charge and thus make it possible for them to go. And we, seeing that state of things, holding in our grasp the relief we had been weeks preparing and organizing in anticipation of this, to turn back, draw off our helpers, send back the doctors already started, give all up because somebody had said something, the press had circulated it, the world had believed it, our disappointed committees had lost heart and grown sore struggling with an occupation rather new to them, and the people had taken alarm and failed to sustain them. Was this all there was of us? No purpose of our own? "On Change," like the price of wheat on the market? In the name of God and Humanity this field must be carried, these people must be rescued; skill, care, medicines and food for the sick must reach them. And it is a glad sight to my soul to think of Turkish troops taking these bands of doctors on to Marash. They have done it, and are at this very hour marching on with them to their field of labor. What does one care for criticism, disapproval or approval, under circumstances like these? Don't be troubled —we can carry it. We are fair financiers, not dismayed, and God helping, can save our hospitals.

It remains to be said that the remedy was effective. The panic settled away and it is to be hoped that there are few people in any country to-day who do not understand that America's fund was distributed by its own agents, without molestation or advices from the Turkish or any other government.

I have named this incident, not so much as a direct feature of the work of distribution, nor to elicit sympathy, as to point a characteristic of our people and the customs of the times in which we are living, in the hope that reflection may draw from it some lessons for the future. One cannot fail to see how nearly a misguided enthusiasm, desire for sensational news, vital action without thought or reflection, came to the overthrowing of their entire object, the destruction of all that had been, or has since been accomplished for humanity, and the burial of their grand work and hopes in a defeated and disgraceful grave, which, in their confusion, they would never have realized that they had dug for themselves. They are to-day justly proud of their work and the world is proud of them.

Our very limited number of assistants made it necessary that each take a separate charge as soon as possible; and the division at Aintab and the hastening of the first division, under Dr. Hubbell, northeastward to Marash, left the northwestern route through Oorfa and Diarbekir, to Messrs. Wistar and Wood; the objective point for all being Harpoot, where they planned to meet at a certain date. Nothing gave me greater joy than to know they would meet our brave and world-honored countrywoman, Miss Shattuck, isolated, surrounded by want and misery, holding her fort alone, and that something from our hands could go to strengthen hers, emptied by the needs of thousands every day. If they might have still gone to Van, and reached our other heroic, capable and accomplished countrywoman, Dr. Grace Kimball, it would have been an added joy. But the way was long, almost to Ararat; the mountains high and the snows deep; and more than all it seemed that the superb management of her own grand work made help there less needed than at many other less fortunate points. It seemed remarkable that the two expeditions separating at Aintab, on the sixth day of April, with no trace of each other between, should have met at Harpoot on April 29, within three hours of each other; and that when the city turned out *en masse*, with its missionaries in the lead, to meet and welcome Dr. Hubbell and the "Red Cross," that far away in the rear, through masses of people from housetop to street, modestly waited the expedition from Oorfa.

This expedition containing as it did two leading men, again divided, taking between them, as their separate reports show, charges of the relief of two hundred villages of the Harpoot vilayet, and later on Diarbekir, and that by their active provision and distribution of farming implements and cattle and the raising of the hopes and courage of the people, they succeeded in securing the harvest and saving the grain crops of those magnificent valleys.

While this was in progress a dispatch came to me at Constantinople from Dr. Shepard of Aintab, whose tireless hands had done the work of a score of men, saying that fevers, both typhoid and typhus of a most virulent nature had broken out in Arabkir, two or three days north of Harpoot; could I send doctors and help? Passing the word on to Dr. Hubbell at Harpoot, the prompt and courageous action was taken by him which his report will name, but never fully show. It is something to say that from a rising pestilence with a score of deaths daily, in five weeks, himself and his assistants left the city in a normally healthful condition in which it remained at last accounts, the mortality ceasing at once under their care and treatment.

During this time the medical relief for the cities of Zeitoun and Marash was in charge of Dr. Harris, who reached there March 18th. The report of the consuls had placed the daily number of deaths from the four contagious diseases at one hundred. This would be quite probable when it is considered that ten thousand were smitten with the prevailing diseases, and that added to this were the crowded conditions of the patients, by the thousands of homeless refugees who had flocked from their forsaken villages; the lack of all comforts, of air, cleanliness, and a state of prolonged starvation. Dr. Harris' first report to me was that he was obliged to set the soup kettles boiling and feed his patients before medicine could be retained. My reply was a draft for two hundred liras, with the added dispatch: "Keep the pot boiling; let us know your wants." The further reports show from this time an astonishingly small number of deaths. The utmost care was taken by all our expeditions to prevent the spread of the contagion and there is no record of its ever having been carried out of the cities, where it was found, either at Zeitoun, Marash, or Arabkir. Lacking this precaution, it might well have spread throughout all Asia Minor, as was greatly feared by the anxious people. On the 24th of May Dr. Harris reported the disease as overcome. His stay being no longer needed, he returned to his great charge in Tripoli with the record of a medical work and success behind him never surpassed if ever equalled. The lives he had saved were enough to gain Heaven's choicest diadem. Never has America cause to be so justly proud and grateful as when its sons and daughters in foreign lands perform deeds of worth like that.

The appalling conditions at Zeitoun and Marash on the arrival of Dr. Harris, naturally led him to call for more physicians, and the most strenuous efforts were made to procure them, but the conditions of the field were not tempting to medical men. Dr. Post had already sent the last recruit from Beyrout, still he manfully continued his efforts. Smyrna was canvassed through the efforts of our prompt and efficient Consul, Col. Madden, on whom I felt free to make heavy drafts, remembering tenderly as we both did, when we stood together in the Red Cross relief of the Ohio floods of 1884. Failing there, I turned my efforts upon Constantinople. Naturally, we must seek nationalties outside of Armenians. We succeeded in finding four Greek physicians, who were contracted with, and sailed May 11th, through perplexing delays of shipping, taking with them large and useful medical supplies and delicacies for the sick, as well as several large disinfecting machines which were loaned to us by the Turkish Government, Dr. Zavitziano, a Greek physician, who kindly assisted us in many ways, conducting the negotiations. Through unavoidable delays they were able to reach Alexandretta only on May 25th. By this time the fevers had been so far overcome that it was not deemed absolutely necessary for them to proceed to Marash; and after conferring with Dr. Harris, they returned to Constantinople, still remaining under kindly contract without remuneration to go at once if called upon by us even to the facing of cholera, if it gained a foothold in Asia Minor. We should not hesitate to call for the services of these gentlemen even at this distance if they became necessary. This was known as the fifth expedition, which, although performing less service was by far the most difficult to obtain, and the most firmly and legally organized of any.

The closing of the medical fields threw our entire force into the general relief of the vilayet of Harpoot which the relieving missionaries had well named their "bottomless pit," and where we had already placed almost the entire funds of the Boston and Worcester committees.

One will need to read largely between the lines of the modest skeleton reports of our agents in order to comprehend only approximately the work performed by them and set in motion for others to perform. The apathy to which the state of utter nothingness, together with their grief and fear, had reduced the inhabitants was by no means the smallest difficulty to be overcome; and here was realized the great danger felt by all — that of continued almsgiving, lest they settle down into a condition of pauperism, and thus, finally starve from the inability of the world at large to feed them. The presence of a strange body of friendly working people coming thousands of miles to help them, awakened a hope and stimulated the desire to help themselves. It was a new experience that these strangers *dared* to come to them. Although the aforetime home lay a heap of stone and sand, and nothing belonging to it remained, still the land was there and when seed to plant the ground and the farming utensils and cattle were brought to work it with, the faint spirit revived, the weak, hopeless hands unclasped, and the farmer stood on his feet again; and when the cities could no longer provide the spades, hoes, plows, picks, and shovels, and the crude iron and steel to make them was taken to them, the blacksmith found again his fire and forge and traveled weary miles with his bellows on his back. The carpenter again swung his hammer and drew his saw. The broken and scattered spinning wheels and looms from under the storms and debris of winter, again took form and motion, and the fresh bundles of wool, cotton, flax, and hemp, in the waiting widow's hand brought hopeful visions of the revival of industries which should not only clothe but feed.

At length, in early June, the great grain fields of Diarbekir, Farkin and Harpoot valleys, planted the year before, grew golden and bowed their heavy spear-crowned heads in waiting for the sickle. But no sickles were there, no scythes, not even knives, and it was a new and sorry sight for our full-handed American farming men, to see those poor, hard, Asiatic hands, trying by main strength to break the tough straw or pull it by the roots. This state of things could not continue, and their sorrow and pity gave place to joy when they were able to drain the cities of Harpoot and Diarbekir of harvest tools, and turned the work of all the village blacksmiths on to the manufacture of sickles and scythes, and of the flint workers upon the rude threshing machines. They have told me since their return that the pleasantest memories left to them, were of those great valleys of golden grain, bending and falling before the harvesters, men and women, each with the new sharp sickle or scythe—the crude threshing planks, the cattle trampling out the grain, and the gleaners in the rear as in the days of Abraham and Moab. God grant that somewhere among them was a kind hearted king of the harvest who gave orders to let some sheaves fall.

Even while this saving process was going on, another condition no less imperative arose. These fields must be replanted for the coming year, or starvation had been simply delayed. Only the strength of their old time teams of oxen could break up the hard sod and prepare for the Fall sowing. Not an animal—ox, cow, horse, goat or sheep had been left. All had been driven to the Kourdish mountains. When Mr. Wood's telegram came, calling for a thousand oxen for the hundreds of villages, some of which were very large, I thought of our not rapidly swelling bank account, and all that was needed everywhere else, and replied accordingly. But when, in return, came the telegram from the Rev. Dr. Gates, president of Harpoot College, the live, active, practical man of affairs, whose judgment no one could question, saying that the need of oxen was imperative, that unless the ground could be ploughed before it dried and hardened, it could not be done at all, and the next harvest would be lost, and that "Mr. Wood's estimate was moderate," I loosened my grasp on the bank account and directed the financial secretary to send a draft for 5,000 liras ($22,000) to care of Rev. Dr. Gates, Harpoot, to be divided among the three expeditions for the purchase of cattle and the progress of the harvest of 1897.

This draft left something less than $3,000 with us to finish up the field in all other directions. As the sum sent would be immediately applied, the active services of the men would be no longer required, and directions went with the remittance to report in person at Constantinople. Unheard of toil, care, hard riding day and night, with risk of life, were all involved in the carrying out of that order. Among the uncivilized and robber bands of Kourds, the cattle that had been stolen and driven off must be picked up, purchased and brought back to the waiting farmers' field. There were routes so dangerous that a brigand chief was selected by those understanding the situation as the safest escort for our men. Perhaps the greatest danger encountered was in the region of Farkin, beyond Diarbekir, where the official escort had not been waited for, and the levelled musket of the faithless guide told the difference.

At length the task was accomplished. One by one the expeditions closed and withdrew, returning by Sivas and Samsoun and coming out by the Black Sea. By that time it is probable that no one questioned the propriety of their route or longer wondered or cared why they went to Smyrna or Alexandretta, Sivas or Sámsoun. The perplexed frowns of our anxious committees and sympathetic people had long given way to smiles of confidence and approval, and glad hands would have reached far over the waters to meet ours as warmly extended to them.

With the return of the expeditions we closed the field, but contributors will be glad to know that subsequent to this, before leaving Constantinople, funds from both the New York and Boston committees came to us amounting to some $15,000. This was happily placed with Mr. Peet, treasurer of the Board of Foreign Missions at Stamboul, to be used subject to our order, and with our concurrence it is now being employed in the building of little houses in the interior as a winter shelter and protection where all had been destroyed.

The appearance of our men on their arrival at Constantinople confirmed the impression that they had not been recalled too soon. They had gone out through the snows and ice of winter and without change or rest had come back through the scorching suns of midsummer—five months of rough, uncivilized life, faring and sharing with their beasts of burden, well nigh out of communication with the civilized world, but never out of danger, it seemed but just to themselves and to others who might yet need them that change and rest be given them.

Since our entrance upon Turkish soil no general disturbance had taken place. One heard only the low rumbling of the thunder after the storm, the clouds were drifting southward and settling over Crete and Macedonia, and we felt that we might take at least some steps towards home. It was only when this movement commenced that we began to truly realize how deep the roots of friendship, comradeship, confidence, and love had struck back among our newly found friends and countrymen; how much a part of ourselves—educational, humanitarian, and official—their work and interests had become, and surely from them we learned anew the lesson of reciprocity.

Some days of physical rest were needful for the men of the expeditions after reaching Constantinople before commencing another journey of thousands of miles, worn as they were by exposure, hardship, and incessant labor, both physical and mental. This interval of time was, however, mainly employed by them in the preparation of the reports submitted with this, and in attention to the letters which followed them from their various fields, telling of further need but more largely overflowing with gratitude and blessing for what had been done.

For our Financial Secretary and myself there could be neither rest nor respite while we remained at a disbursing post so well known as ours. Indeed there never had been. From the time of our arrival in February to our embarkation in August, there were but two days not strictly devoted to business—the 4th of July and the 5th of August—the last a farewell to our friends. For both of these occasions we were indebted to the hospitality of Treasurer and Mrs. W. W. Peet, and although held in the open air, on the crowning point of Proti, one of the Princes' Islands, with the Marmara, Bosphorus and Golden Horn in full view, the spires and minarets of Constantinople and Scutari telling us of a land we knew little of, with peoples and customs strange and incomprehensible to us, still there was no lack of the emblem that makes every American at home, and its wavy folds of red, white and blue shaded the tables and flecked the tasteful viands around which sat the renowned leaders of the American missionary element of Asia Minor. Henry O. Dwight, D. D., the accomplished gentleman and diplomatic head, who was the first to suggest an appeal to the Red Cross, and I am glad to feel he has never repented him of his decision. One fact in regard to Dr. Dwight may be of interest to some hundreds of thousands of our people: On first meeting him I was not quite sure of the title by which to address him, if reverend or doctor, and took the courage to ask him. He turned a glance full of amused meaning upon me as he replied: "That is of little consequence; the title I prize most is *Captain* Dwight." "Of what?" I asked. "Co. D, 20th Ohio Volunteers in our late war." The recognition which followed can well be imagined by the comrades for whose interest I have named the incident.

Rev. Joseph K. Greene, D. D., and his amiable wife, to whom so much is due towards the well being of the missionary work of Constantinople. I regret that I am not able to reproduce the eloquent and patriotic remarks of Dr. Greene on both these occasions, so true to our country, our Government and our laws. Rev. George P. Knapp, formerly of Bitlis, whose courage no one questions. Mrs. Lee of Marash, and Mrs. Dr. George Washburn of Robert College, the worthy and efficient daughters of Rev. Dr. Cyrus Hamlin, the veteran missionary and founder of Robert College, living in Lexington, Mass. A half-score of teachers, whose grand lives will one day grace the pages of religious history. And last, though by no means least, our host, the man of few words and much work, who bears the burden of monetary relief for the woes and wants of Asia Minor, W. W. Peet, Esq.

It was a great satisfaction that most of our field agents were able to be present at the last of these beautiful occasions and personally render an account of their stewardship to those who had watched their course with such interest. The pleasure of these two days of recreation will ever remain a golden light in our memories.

As the first official act of the relief work after our arrival in Constantinople was my formal presentation to the Sublime Porte by the American minister, Hon. A. W. Terrell, diplomatic courtesy demanded that I take proper occasion to notify the Turkish Government of our departure and return thanks for its assistance, which was done formally at "Selamlic," a religious ceremony held on the Turkish Sabbath which corresponds to our Friday. The Court Chamberlain delivered my message to the palace. It was received and responded to through the same medium and I took my departure, having finished my diplomatic work with that Government which had from first to last treated me with respect, assisted my work and protected my workers.

To correct certain impressions and expressions which have been circulating more or less extensively in this country, and for the correct information of the people who through their loyal interest deserve to know the facts, I make known my entire social relations while residing in Turkey. Personally I did not go beyond Constantinople. The proper conduct of our work demanded the continuous presence of both our Financial Secretary and myself at headquarters. I never saw, to personally communicate with, any member of the Turkish Government excepting its Minister of Foreign Affairs, Tewfik Pasha, as named previously. I never spoke with the Sultan and have never seen him excepting in his carriage on the way to his mosque.

On being informed through our Legation that the Turkish minister at Washington, Mavroyeni Bey, had been recalled and that his successor was about to leave for his new position, I felt that national courtesy required that I call upon him and, attended by a member of our legation, my secretary and myself crossed the Bosphorus to a magnificent estate on the Asiatic shore, the palatial home of Moustapha Tahsin Bey, a gentleman of culture, who had resided in New York in some legal capacity and who, I feel certain, will be socially and officially acceptable to our Government.

I have never received from the Turkish Government any decoration or other testimonial of approval, although that is its customary and usual method of expressing public satisfaction. If later any such expression of approval of the relief sent by our country be given I will make it known, as due to the generosity of our people and by no means personal for myself.

I have, however, received a decoration, officially described as follows:

"Brevet of Chevalier of the Royal Order of Melusine, founded in 1186, by Sibylle, Queen and spouse of King Guy of Jerusalem, and re-instituted several years since by Marie, Princess of Lusignan. The order is conferred for humanitarian, scientific and other services of distinction, but especially when such services are rendered to the House of Lusignan, and particularly to the Armenian Nation. The Order is worn by a number of reigning sovereigns, and is highly prized by the recipients because of its rare bestowal and its beauty. This decoration is bestowed by His Royal Highness, Guy of Lusignan, Prince of Jerusalem, Cyprus and Armenia."

The first notice of this honor came to me through our own Smithsonian Institute, as indicating its scientific character.

On the ninth of August we took passage on board the S. S. "Meteor," a Roumanian steamer plying between Constantinople and the ports of the Black Sea, our objective point being Costanza at the mouth of the Danube River. This was our first step toward home, and the leaving of a people on whom, in common with the civilized world, our whole heart interest had been centered for more than half a year; having no thought, however, until the hour of parting revealed it, of the degree of interest that had been centered on us.

On the spacious deck of the steamer were assembled our entire American representation at Constantinople, prepared to accompany us through the Bosphorus, their boats having been sent forward to take them off near the entrance of the Black Sea.

The magnificent new quay in either direction was crowded with people without distinction of nationality, the strange costumes and colors commingling in such variety as only an Oriental city can produce, patiently waiting the long hour of preparation. When at length the hoarse whistle sounded and the boat swayed from its moorings, the dense crowd swayed with it and the subdued tones pealed out in tongues many and strange; but all had one meaning—thanks, blessings and God speed. We received these manifestations reverently, for while they meant kindliness to us and our work, they meant far more of homage and honor for the nation and people we represented. And not only in Constantinople but the shores of the Bosphorus as we proceeded, presented similar tokens of recognition—the wavy Stars and Stripes from Robert College, Bebek, and Hissar, told more strongly than words how loyal to their own free land were the hearts and hands toiling so faithfully in others.

Touching at Budapest for a glimpse at its Millennial Exposition; at Vienna to pay respects to our worthy Minister, Hon. Bartlett Tripp; we hastened to meet the royal greeting of the Grand Duke and Grand Duchess of Baden, at their beautiful island of Minau in Lake Constance—the wedding gift of the Grand Duke to his young princess bride forty-three years ago. It was a great pleasure to be able to bring our hard-worked men into personal contact with these active royal personages, who know so well in their own philanthropic lives how to appreciate such labor in others.

Lest some may not recall directly the lines of royal succession, our readers will pardon me if I say that the Grand Duchess of Baden is the only daughter of the old Emperor William and Empress Augusta, the sister of Germany's "Fritz," the aunt of the present Emperor, the mother of the Crown Princess of Sweden, and the granddaughter of the beloved Queen Louise, whom she is said to very much resemble.

One day was given to Strassburg—another labor field of the Franco-German war, of longer duration than Armenia—reaching London on the 24th day of August.

Our passage was engaged on the "Servia," to sail September 1st, when the news of the terrible troubles in Constantinople reached us. We were shocked and distressed beyond words. The streets where we had passed, the people who had served us, the Ottoman bank where we had transacted business almost daily for nearly half a year, all in jeopardy if not destroyed. Our men of the interior feared a general uprising there, in which case we might be able to help. Our sense of duty did not permit us to proceed until the facts were better known. We cancelled or rather transferred our passage by the "Servia," telegraphed to Constantinople and cabled to America, expressing our willingness to return to the field if our services were in any way needed. Kindly advices from both directions, together with a more quiet condition of things, decided us to continue our journey, and engaging passage by the "Umbria" for the 5th, we arrived in New York on the 12th of September, eight months lacking ten days from the time of our departure on the 22d of January.

DISTANCES AND DIFFICULTIES OF TRAVEL, TRANSPORTATION AND COMMUNICATIONS.

For the convenience of the closely occupied who have not time to study as they read, I have thought it well to condense the information above referred to in a paragraph, which can be taken in at a glance, in connection with the map.

The one great port of Asia Minor, is Constantinople. To reach the center, known as Anatolia or Armenia, there are two routes from Constantinople. One by way of the Mediterranean sea to Alexandretta, the southern port or gateway; the other by the Black Sea, to reach the northern ports of Samsoun and Trebizond, lying along the southern coast of the Black Sea. There is no land route, but a "pony post," like the overland days of California, takes important dispatches for the government, or money. The way is infested by brigands.

There are no regular passenger boats, but Russia, Austria, France and Greece have despatch—in reality, coasting boats, one of which aims to leave Constantinople each week, although at first we found it at least two weeks between the times of sailing and irregular at that.

The time from Constantinople to Alexandretta is eight to ten days. From Constantinople to Samsoun, two days. From either of these ports the interior must be reached by land.

From Alexandretta to Harpoot is fifteen (15) days.
" " " Marash is five (5) days.
" " " Zeitoun is seven (7) days.
" " " Oorfa is six (6) days.
" " " Diarbekir is twelve (12) days.

On the north from Samsoun to Harpoot is fifteen (15) days.

These journeys were made by horse, mule or donkey, over mountain paths, rocks and precipices. Only in comparatively a few places are there roads allowing the passing of a wheeled vehicle of any kind, even the passing of a horse along the steep declivities is sometimes dangerous.

COMMUNICATIONS.

As will be seen, the sending of a letter from Constantinople to the interior, requires at the best six weeks, or forty-six days with no delays.

Only the large and more important towns have telegraphic communication. This requires two, three, four days or a week, according to circumstances. These despatches are all sent and must be answered in Turkish. The larger towns have mails usually leaving once a week, carried on horses with a military guard. No newspaper is published in Asia Minor.

The missionary stations, with but two or three exceptions, are not near the seacoast, but from three to fifteen days travel from either the Mediterranean or the Black Sea, or three to twenty-five days to the nearest Mediterranean port. As will be seen by reference to the map the following stations are on the seaboard: Trebizond on the Black Sea; Smyrna and a small station near Merisine on the Mediterranean, and Constantinople on the Bosphorus.

The following are inland and during several months in the winter and spring must be nearly, if not quite, inaccessible to outside approach: Adabazar, Bardezag, Brousa, Cesarea, Marsovan, Hadjin, Tarsus, Adana, Mardin, Aintab, Marash, Sivas, Harpoot, Oorfa, Erzingan, Erzroom, Van, Bitlis.

FUNDS.

It should be distinctly understood by contributors, that neither their letters, nor any individual contributions came to us; these were received by the committees or parties raising the funds in America. The letters were doubtless faithfully acknowledged, and the various sums of money placed in the general fund forwarded to us by them. All contributions received by us directly at Constantinople are acknowledged in our report.

Although an account of the disposition of all funds is rendered in the report of the financial secretary, which, after verification, I signed jointly with him, I will however at the risk of repetition, take the liberty of adding the following remarks on the subject:

It is to be borne always in mind that the *amount* of money to be distributed was never made a concern of ours, provided there were actually "*funds to distribute.*" To the question so frequently and kindly asked of us, "Did you have money enough, or were you embarrassed in your operations by want of funds?" I beg to have this reply intelligently understood; that we had always money enough in hand for the work in hand. We were never embarrassed in our operations by lack of funds, holding as I always have, that charitable relief in order to be safe and efficient, should be conducted on the same reasonable basis as business, and that a good business man unless by accident on the part of other persons, or of circumstances, will never find himself embarrassed, as he will never undertake more than he has the means to successfully accomplish. We were never embarassed in our operations by lack of funds, and our committees will testify that no intimation of that kind ever came to them from us. This would have been both unwise and unjust. According to the universal system of charitable relief, all was being done that could be done; but if asked if we had enough for the *needs of the people*, enough to relieve the distress through desolated Asia Minor, enough to make those people comfortable again, then a very tender chord has been touched. No hearts in America are more sore than ours; its richest mine might drain in that attempt. Our men in the interior have seen and lived among what others vainly strive to picture; they are men of work not words, and under Heaven have labored to do what they could with what they had. It is their stewardship they are trying to render to a great-hearted, sympathetic and perplexed people, racked by various emotions, seeking light through every channel, and conclusively solving and settling in a score of ways, every day, problems and questions which have unsettled a considerable portion of the world for centuries.

THE COMMITTEES.

On behalf of the wrechedness and suffering met through Asia Minor, we return heartfelt thanks to the committees who labored with such untiring zeal toward their relief. We were never unmindful of the difficulties which they were constantly called to encounter and to overcome. Not having in hand the funds desired or even guaranteed, they must raise them, and this largely from persons whose sympathies outran their generosity, if not their means. This naturally opened the door for excuses for withholding, until it could be seen that "something was actually being accomplished;" then the doubt if anything "could be accomplished;" next the certainty that it "could not be," and so on through whole chapters of dark prophecies and discouragements sufficient to dishearten the most hopeful natures, and weaken at times the best efforts that could be put forth. Against volumes, nay, oceans of these discouragements, our committees must have struggled, with more or less of success, and again for their efforts on behalf of such suffering as even they never witnessed, we return with reverence our sincerest gratitude. Their efforts have been herculean, their obstructions scarcely less.

The cause of these difficulties lay in the customary conception and methods of charitable relief, which they were naturally compelled to adopt and follow. Until the world comes to recognize that charity is not beggary, and should not be made to depend upon it, that a legitimate and ready fund to draw from in order to facilitate and validate its transactions is as necessary as in other movements, the difficulties of our tireless and noble committees will be everywhere met.

It is with these views that the Red Cross has never solicited means in aid of its work of relief. Heretofore on all its fields, the people have been left free to contribute what they desired, and through whom they desired, and it is we believe, a well understood fact, that the use of the name of the Red Cross in the raising of funds for the late Armenian relief, was simply incidental, one of the methods naturally resorted to in order to secure the end, and by no concurrence of ours, as has been previously and fully explained.

TO THE PRESS OF THE UNITED STATES.

Among the dark hours that came to us in the hopeless waste of work and woe on every side, the strong sustaining power has been the Press of the United States. While naturally compelled to give circulation to unauthorized reports from other sources, it has evidently done it with regret, and hastened by strong editorials, in words of no uncertain sound, to set right before its readers any errors that may have crept in. The American press has always been loyal to the Red Cross and to its work, and once more it is our privilege to tender to it our meed of grateful praise.

TO THE CONTRIBUTORS OF THE UNITED STATES;

Whose sympathy, God-like pity and mercy prompted them to the grand work of relief for the half million suffering and dying in a land they had never seen, whose purses were opened, whose own desires were repressed that they might give, not of their abundance, but of their scantiness ofttimes, whose confidence made us their almoners, whose whole-hearted trust has strengthened us, whose hearts have been with us, whose prayers have followed us, whose hopes have sustained us, and whose beckoning hands were held out in tenderness to welcome us back to them, what can be said, what can be done, but to bow our heads in grateful recognition of the words of unexpected commendation which nearly overwhelm us, and pray the gracious God that He bless our work, to the measure of the praise bestowed.

TO OUR GOVERNMENT AT WASHINGTON;

To its cordial sympathy so warmly expressed through its honored Secretaries of State and Navy, and through whose ready access we were at all times able to reach the public, our earnest and respectful thanks are rendered, begging our warm-hearted people to bear in mind that our rulers are a part of, and like themselves; that the security of the government lies largely in the fact that responsibility tends to conservatism—not necessarily less sympathetic, but less free, more responsible and more thoughtful.

TO OUR LEGATION IN CONSTANTINOPLE.

Our thanks are due to our genial minister, Hon. A. W. Terrell, his accomplished secretary, and *charges d'affairs*, J. W. Riddle, his interpreter and dragoman, Gargiulo, our Consul General, Luther Short, Esq., the consular interpreter, Demetriades, from every one of whom we received unremitting care and attention during all the months of our residence at Constantinople, and without which aid we could not have succeeded in our work. There was not an hour that their free service was not placed at our command. Through them all governmental business was transacted. The day was never too long nor the night too short for any active help they could render; I only hope that our diplomatic service at all courts is as faithfully and cheerfully rendered as at Constantinople. In this connection I desire to make special mention of the assistance of U. S. Consul, Dr. Milo A. Jewett, at Sivas, and Consular Agent, Daniel Walker, at Alexandretta.

Both personally and officially I believe the record of Minister Terrell will sustain him. While firm and direct of speech he is a man of uncommon courtesy, abounding in the old time hospitality of his native state, Virginia. If at the close of his official term, he shall be able to report that through all the months—nay, years of unheard-of troubles, dangers and deaths in the country to which he was assigned, while some hundreds of his fellow citizens were constantly and peculiarly exposed to these dangers, that with no direct governmental aid or authority, without even a ship of his own country in port, that no life in his charge has been lost, and that only such dangers, hardship and losses as were incident to the terrible transactions about them had been inflicted upon them, we will, I trust, look calmly at the results, and decide that if this were not diplomacy, it was a very good substitute.

TO THE AMBASSADORS OF OTHER NATIONS AT CONSTANTINOPLE.

To these high and honorable gentlemen our thanks are due. To Sir Philip Currie of England, there seemed to come no difference in sentiment between our people and his own; a tower of strength wherever he took hold. Germany and Russia were cordial and ready to aid, as also our English Consul, R. A. Fontana, at Harpoot, and C. M. Hallward, at Diarbekir; and following these, may I also name the ready help of Reuter's Express and the United and Associated Presses of both Constantinople and London.

COMMENDATORY.

Here is a phase of our work which should not be entirely passed by, and yet, if only partially taken up would overrun our entire report. Only one or two excerpts must suffice to show what the others might mean.

From Rev. Dr. H. O. Dwight, one word among the many so generously spoken:

"Miss Barton has done a splendid work, sensibly and economically managed. Wherever her agents have been, the missionaries have expressed the strongest approval of their methods and efficiency. The work done has been of great and permanent importance."

Rev. Joseph K. Greene, D. D.:

"After some six months of service Miss Clara Barton and her five able assistants have left Constantinople on their return to America. It was only on the earnest solicitation of the missionaries, the officers of the American Board and many other friends of the suffering Armenians that Miss Barton undertook the relief in this land. The difficulties of the work, arising from the suspicions of the Turkish authorities, the distance from the capital to the sufferers, the perils and discomforts in communicating with them, and from unfamiliarity with the languages and customs of the people of the land would surely have appalled a less courageous heart. Under such circumstances it is only just and fair that the American public should be apprised of the substantial success of this mission of the Red Cross.

"In the first place, Miss Barton has shown a rare faculty in getting on well with everybody. To facilitate her work she, and the assistants whom she loves to call "my men," laid aside all the insignia of the Red Cross and appeared everywhere simply as private individuals. She clearly understood that she could accomplish her mission only by securing the confidence and good will of the authorities, and this she did by her patience and repeated explanations, and by the assistance of the American Legation. When the *iradé*, or imperial decree sanctioning her mission was delayed, she sent forward her assistants with only a traveling permit for a part of the way, trusting and not in vain, that the local authorities, instructed from headquarters, would facilitate their way. As a matter of fact, while Mr. Pullman, her secretary and treasurer, remained at Constantinople with Miss Barton, her distributing agents, namely, Dr. Hubbell and Mr. Mason, Mr. Wistar and Mr. Wood, either together or in two parties, traveled inland from Alexandretta to Killis, Aintab, Marash, Zeitun, Birejik, Oorfa, Diarbekir, Farkin, Harpoot, Palou, Malatia, Arabkir, Egin, Sivas, Tokat, Samsoun and back to Constantinople without interruption or molestation. They were readily and constantly supplied with guards, and could not with safety have made their perilous four months' journey without them. Demands are said to have been made that the distribution of aid be made under the supervision of Government officials, but in fact, Miss Barton's agents knew how to make their distributions in every place, after careful consultation and examination, without any interferance on the part of the authorities.

"Miss Barton received in all, about $116,000, and an unexpended balance of $15,400 was committed to Mr. Peet, the treasurer of the American Missions in Turkey, to be held as an emergency fund, subject to Miss Barton's orders. No expense has been incurred for Miss Barton or her agents save for traveling expenses and the wages of interpreters, and with this exception the entire sum expended has gone to the actual relief of the sufferers. While the fund committed to the Anglo-American Committee, of which Mr. Peet is a member—a sum four to five times the amount committed to Miss Barton—has been expended through the missionaries, largely to save the hungry from starvation, the relief through the agents of the Red Cross has for the most part, been wisely devoted to the putting of the poor sufferers on their feet again and thus helping them to help themselves. Some 500 liras (a lira is $4.40 of *good* money) were given for the cure and care of the sick in Marash, Zeitoun and elsewhere, and some 2,000 liras' worth of cloths, thread, pins and needles were sent inland; but many times this amount was expended in providing material for poor widows, seeds, agricultural implements and oxen for farmers; tools for blacksmiths and carpenters, and looms for weavers. In some places Miss Barton's agents had the pleasure of seeing vegetable gardens coming forward from seed furnished by the Red Cross, and village farmers reaping the grain with sickles which the Red Cross had given. The great want now—a want which the funds of the Red Cross agents did not permit them to any large extent to meet—is aid to the poor villagers to help them rebuild their burned and ruined houses, and thus provide for themselves shelter against the rigors of the coming winter. The Red Cross agents have however, gathered a great stock of information; and passing by the horrors of the massacres and the awful abuse of girls and women, as unimpeachable witnesses they can bear testimony to the frightful sufferings and needs of the people. We most sincerely hope and pray that Miss Barton and the agents and friends of the Red Cross will not esteem their work in Turkey done, but knowing now so well just what remains to be done, and what can be done, will bend every effort to secure further relief for the widows and orphans of the more than sixty thousand murdered men—mostly between the ages of eighteen and fifty—whose lives no earthly arm was outstretched to save.

"While we gratefully bear witness to the wise and indefatigable efforts of Miss Barton's *agents*, permit us to add that during her more than six months' stay in Constantinople Miss Barton gave *herself* unremittingly to the work of her mission. She seems to have had no time for sight-seeing, and not a few of her friends are disposed to complain that she had no time to accept the invitations of those who would have been glad to enter-

REV. JOSEPH K. GREENE, D. D., CONSTANTINOPLE.

CEREMONY OF "SALAMLIC."

THE OUTER OR PERA BRIDGE ACROSS THE GOLDEN HORN
CONNECTING STAMBOUL WITH GALATA.

tain her. The only relaxation she seems to have given herself was on two occasions—the first, a Fourth of July picnic with a few American friends, on one of the Princes' Islands, and the second, another picnic on the same island, on Wednesday, August 5th when, with three of her "men," she met some twenty American lady teachers and missionaries, in order to bid them a courteous farewell. The first occasion she unqualifiedly declared to have been the happiest Fourth of July she had ever had; and inspired by the occasion, she penned some verses which she kindly read to her friends on the second gathering, and which we very much wish she would permit the editor of *The Independent* to publish. On the second occasion, at Miss Barton's request, Mr. Pullman read his financial report and Dr. Hubbell and Mr. Wood presented reports of the work of distribution. We gratefully acknowledged the honor done us in permitting us to hear these reports; and, remembering our concern for Miss Barton while preparing for the work of distribution six months ago, we gladly expressed our joy and congratulations now on the happy return of her faithful and efficient agents, of whom it may be truly said that they went and saw and conquered. We rejoiced that these new friends had come to know so well the American missionaries in Turkey, and were truly thankful for a mutually happy acquaintance. We wished Miss Barton and her "men" a hearty welcome on their arrival, and now, with all our hearts, we wish them god-speed on their return home."

Constantinople, Turkey.

The little "verses" so kindly referred to by Dr. Greene, were not even written, but were a simple train of thought that took rythmic form as we crossed over the sea of Marmara, on our way to an island celebration of the 4th of July. Later I found time to put them on paper and read them to the guests at our farewell meeting, presenting them to our host, Mr. W. W. Peet. They appear to have gained a favor far beyond their merit, and by request of many friends they are given place in the report as a "part of its history."

MARMARA.

It was twenty and a hundred years, oh blue and rolling sea,
A thousand in the onward march of human liberty,
Since on its sunlit bosom, wind tossed and sails unfurled,
Atlantic's mighty billows bore a message to the world.

It thunders down its rocky coast, and stirs its frugal homes;
The Saxon hears it as he toils, the Indian as he roams;
The buffalo upon the plains, the panther in his lair,
And the eagle hails the kindred note, and screams it through the air.

"Make way for liberty," it roared, "here let the oppressed go free,
Break loose your bands of tyrant hands, this land is not for thee.
The old world in its crusted grasp, grinds out the souls of men,
Here plant their feet in freedom's soil, this land was made for them."

The mother slept in her island home, but the children heard the call,
And 'ere the western sun went down, had answered, one and all;
For Britain's thirteen colonies had vanished in a day,
And six and half a hundred men had signed their lives away.

And brows were dark, and words were few, the steps were quick and strong,
And firm the lips as ever his who treasures up a wrong;
And stern the tone that offered up the prayer beside the bed,
And many a Molly Stark that night, wept silent tears of dread.

The bugles call, and swords are out, and armies march abreast,
And the old world casts a wondering glance to the strange light in the west;
Lo, from its lurid lightnings play, free tossing in the wind,
Bursts forth the star-gemmed flag that wraps the hopes of all mankind.

And weary eyes grew brighter then, and fainting hearts grew strong,
And hope was mingled in the cry, "How long, oh Lord, how long?"
The seething millions turn and stir and struggle towards the light;
The free flag streams, and morning gleams where 'erst was hopeless night.

And grim Atlantic thunders still, adown its rocky shores,
And still the eagle screams his note, as aloft he sails and soars;
And hope is born, that even thou, in some far day to come,
Oh blue and rolling Marmara, shalt bear the message home.

  Dedicated to W. W. Peet, Esq.   Clara Barton.
Constantinople. July 4th, 1896.

Reports are always tedious. If some reader, having persevered thus far, if such there be, shall find himself or herself saying with a little thrill of disappointment, "But this does not give the information expected, it does not recommend any specific course to be pursued, whether emmigration for the Armenians, and if so, where, and how; or Autonomy, and if so, how to be secured, and assured; if more ships should be sent, and what they should do when there; if greater pressure of the Powers should be demanded by us, or what course, as a nation, we ought to pursue. We had expected some light on these questions."

Appreciating and regretting this disappointment, we must remind our anxious readers and friends—for such they are—that we have never been required to do this; that all conclusions to that effect, are simply inferential, and all such expectations were born of anxious hope. But that which we feel *does* immediately concern us, and comes directly within our province, is, to state that notwithstanding all that has been done through all sources, infinitely more remains to be done by some one; and while speculation upon the moral duty of nations, the rights or wrongs of governments, the problem of whether one ruler or another shall sit upon a throne for the next six months; what expressions of individual principle in regard to certain actions should be given; the proper stand for a people to take and maintain on high moral and religious questions—all important subjects—none value them more than I—all marking the high tone and progressive spirit of the most advanced stage of human thought and culture the world has yet known, it would seem that each and all of these, imperative and important as they are, admit of at least a little moment of time for consideration, and will probably take it whether admitted or not.

But the facts are, that between the Archipelago and the Caspian Seas, the Black and the Mediterranean, are to-day living a million and a half of people of the Armenian race, existing under the ordinances of, at least, semi-civilization, and professing the religion of Jesus Christ; that according to the stated estimate of intelligent and impartial observers of various countries and concurred in by our own agents, whose observations have been unrestricted, from 100,000 to 200,000 of these persons, men, women and children, are destitute of shelter, raiment, fire, food, medicines, the comforts that tend to make human life preservable, or any means of obtaining them, save through the charitable beneficence of the world.

The same estimates concur in the statement, that without such outside support, at least 50,000 of these persons will have died of starvation or perished through accumulated hardship, before the first of May, 1897.

That even now it is cold in their mountain recesses, the frosts are whitening the rocky crests, trodden by their wandering feet, and long before Christmas the friendly snow will have commenced to cover their graves.

These facts, bare and grim, are what I have to present to the American people; and if it should be proposed to make any use of them there is not much time for consideration. We have hastened, without loss of a day, to bring them plainly and truthfully before the public as a subject pertaining peculiarly to it.

I would like to add that this great work of human relief should not fall *wholly* upon the people of our own country—by no means without its own suffering poor—neither would it. The people of most enlightened nations should unite in this relief, and I believe, properly conferred with, would do so.

None of us have found any better medium for the dispensation of charitable relief than the faithful missionaries already on the ground, and our Government officers, whose present course bespeaks their active interest.

CLARA BARTON.

REPORT OF

GEORGE H. PULLMAN,

FINANCIAL SECRETARY OF THE AMERICAN

NATIONAL RED CROSS.

The following financial report, of necessity, has to deal with the currencies of five different countries, viz.: American, English, French, Austrian, and Turkish, but as nearly all except expenses of travel and maintenance are in Turkish money, and as American, English, French, and other moneys received were naturally reduced to the coin of the Ottoman Empire, we were obliged to make our accounts to correspond. As the report is made on the gold basis of 100 piasters to a lira, our friends may easily find the value in American money by multiplying the number of piasters by 4.4, as a gold lira (100 piasters) is approximately worth four and four-tenths dollars.

Owing to the difference in values between gold and silver coin, the wide range of values between the same coin in different cities, also the singular variation of the purchasing power of the same coin in the same cities for various commodities, complicated and curious mathematical problems have constantly confronted us, and for the correctness and accuracy of our report we are under many obligations to W. W. Peet, Esq., treasurer of the American Board of Foreign Missions; the officers of the Imperial Ottoman and Credit Lyonnais Banks; as well as George Künzel, Esq., expert accountant of the Administration de la Dette Publique Ottomane. Our grateful acknowledgments are also due and heartily given to Rev. Dr. H.

O. Dwight, the executive head of the Missionary Board at Constantinople, and Rev. Dr. George Washburn, president of Robert College, for many valuable suggestions.

To give a single illustration of the acrobatic acquirements of the sprightly piaster, the ignus fatuus characteristics of the mejidieh (nom. 20 piasters), and the illusive proclivities of the lira, we will outline a transaction connected with our first medical expedition, under Dr. Ira Harris, of Tripoli, Syria. We had sent four hundred liras to Dr. George E. Post, of Beyrout, who was fitting out the expedition for us, and presumed we would receive a receipt for that amount, or for 40,000 piasters, its equivalent. The acknowledgment came, and we were somewhat nonplussed to note that we had been credited with a sum far exceeding that amount. A letter of inquiry was sent, as we supposed our good doctor had made an error. We quote a a paragraph or two in his letter of reply: "I am not surprised that you do not quite understand the intricacies of Turkish finance. After thirty-three years of residence, I am still trying to get some idea of what a piaster is. * * * In Beyrout it is worth one piaster and five paras, with variations; a mejidieh is worth from nineteen piasters to almost anything. Every town has its rate. * * * The nominal value changes daily. Thus if I credit you to-day with 123.20 piasters on the lira, next week I may be out of pocket, or vice versa. * * * Internally, it is well nigh impossible to keep accounts. * * * The only way our college books are kept is by giving the rate as it is when the account is entered and as it appears in all receipts and other vouchers."

We were much gratified with this assurance, for if a college president, after thirty-three years study had not solved the piaster puzzle, there was some excuse for us. Hundreds of accounts and bills have been received, audited and paid, and scarcely any two correspond in piaster equivalents. Therefore, although the money unit is the gold piaster, and the monetary standard the gold lira, the frequent changes in valuation is very bewildering to foreigners, and necessitates frequent conference with persons who, after long years of residence, have reached an equitable basis by which monetary equivalents can be ascertained.

A glance at our column of receipts shows a considerable variation in rates of exchange, and also the selling price of British gold (most of our drafts and cabled credits were in English sovereigns). We sold the greater part of our gold at a rate exceeding 110, which is the commercial rate in business transactions. In all credits received, the values are of course given according to the rate on the day of sale.

Many of our accounts, receipts and vouchers are curiosities, as they are in various languages, Arabic, Kourdish, Turkish, Armenian, Greek, Italian, etc. They were interesting but at the same time exceedingly perplexing to us, though our expert accountant found no difficulty with any of them, and right here we desire to make special acknowledgment to Mr. Künzel for his excellent but unpaid services.

In our column of expenses will be found an exceedingly rare Red Cross item, namely, "Wages Account." All the native or local doctors and apothecaries with one exception, had to be paid "contagious disease rates," as they called it. The exception was Dr. Ira Harris, of Tripoli, Syria, that brave and self-sacrificing American, whose great medical ability and splendid surgical skill accomplished so much in curing the sick in the terribly distressed cities of Marash and Zeitoun, with their many surrounding villages. We are glad to make this public acknowledgment in full appreciation of his heroic services. Beside the doctors, there were interpreters and dragomen for the various expeditions in the field to whom wages were paid. No adverse reflection is designed in the making of this statement, as the conditions surrounding life and service in that region of operation made such remuneration an equitable necessity.

It is, we think, a well understood fact, that the Red Cross officers neither receive nor ask any remuneration for their services, but away from our own country we did not find the splendid volunteer aids we have had on former fields. But few could be found, and these we have had with us both in Constantinople and Asia Minor, and very efficient helpers they have been; to these our thanks are due and cordially given.

After our expeditions had entered the field and begun work, the first remittances to our chief officers were sent in a manner which for slowness and seeming insecurity would have appalled American business men. The *modus operandi* was as follows: A check for the amount desired was drawn and taken to the bank; after half an hour or more the gold would be weighed out and handed over — our bankers would have performed the same service in two minutes. The coin was then put into a piece of stout canvas cloth, done up in a round ball, securely tied, and taken to the Imperial Turkish post office where it was placed in a piece of sheepskin, all the ends brought together very evenly, cut off square and covered with sealing wax, the strong cords binding the package in a peculiar manner were woven in so that the ends could be passed through a small wooden box like a pill box; this box was filled with wax. After the Imperial Post and our seals were attached, bakshish given, and the package insured in an English company, the only thing remaining after the three or four hours work and delay was to go home and with fear and trembling wait some twenty-five or thirty days until the pony express arrived at its destination and an acknowledgment by telegraph of the receipt of the money relieved the nervous strain as far as *that* package was concerned. This trying business was kept up until it became possible to use drafts in the interior. We are happy to report that though the money had to be taken through a country infested with robbers, outlaws, and brigands, we never lost a lira.

Bakshish is another custom of the country, infinitely more exasperating than our "tip" system, which is bad enough.

REV. HENRY O. DWIGHT, D. D.

W. W. PEET, ESQ.

SUBLIME PORTE, STAMBOUL.

VIEW FROM RED CROSS HEADQUARTERS, SHOWING GOLDEN HORN, BOSPHORUS AND MARMARA.

This is trying to most people but peculiarly irritating to a financial secretary. Bakshish is a gift of money which an Oriental expects and demands for the most trifling service. Beggars, by instinct, seem to know a financial secretary. and swarm around in the most appalling manner. To make any headway with this horde at least two Turkish words must be mastered the first day, namely " *Yok*"—No, and "*Hidi-git*"—Be off with you. These expressions are sometimes efficacious with beggars but the bakshish fiend must be paid something.

As long columns of figures have no interest to the great majority of people, and detailed accounts of receipts and expenses are never read, as it is of no possible importance what moneys were received at certain times, or what goods were purchased on specific days for the field work, or gold or drafts sent into the interior, we give our statement in as condensed a form as possible. The committees have received their respective reports, with all vouchers and other detail.

We believe the account of our stewardship will be approved by our countrymen; we know that the people whom we came to assist, are grateful and thoroughly appreciative, as numberless letters of gratitude, testimonials and personal statements abundantly prove.

To the $116,326.01, at least a third if not a half more should be added, as in all kinds of industrial business we have made the money do double duty. For instance: we purchased iron and steel and gave to the blacksmiths to make tools. That started their work. They paid us for the iron and steel in tools; these we gave to other artisans to start their various trades. In like manner spinning, weaving and garment-making avocations were commenced. Speaking of values, the consensus of opinion of our countrymen in the interior is, that putting a price on our work, the people of Anatolia have gained twice or thrice the actual money spent, and that the moral support given was far beyond any valuation. (At such a money valuation then, the aggregate value of the relief distribution will be nearly $350,000.)

A few words of explanation in regard to the table of expenditures: "Cash sent to the Interior" includes all moneys sent by pony express or draft, and of this amount something over seven thousand liras are in the hands of W. W. Peet, Esq.; Rev. C. F. Gates, at Harpoot; C. M. Hallward, Esq., British Consul, at Diarbekir; Rev. E. H. Perry, at Sivas, and other equally responsible representatives, for an emergency fund, to be used, on order, as occasion requires.

"Relief Expeditions, General and Medical," represent largely the goods purchased and shipped with the four expeditions from Constantinople and Beyrout for relief purposes. A portion of this supply is still held at different stations awaiting the proper time for its distribution to the best advantage.

"General Expense Account" represents freights, postage, bakshish, hammals, car fares, carriages, etc. "Donations for Relief of Orphan Children" represents sums of money given to the Armenian and German hospitals for Armenian refugee children. The other items we think explain themselves.

It will be observed that the special Red Cross fund, as noted in our tabulation of debits and credits, more than covers expenses of "Red Cross Headquarters, Field," "Travel and Maintenance," "General Expense and Wages Accounts," and "General and Medical Relief Expeditions Accounts," all of which items were of direct benefit to the field as all were necessary to the successful conduct of our work. We only mention this to show that, besides the work we have been able to successfully perform, the Red Cross has also materially contributed monetarily to the field. And it will not be out of place to note that in the total of cash expended ($116,326.01) there is shown to be an administrative cost amounting to $7,526.37, as covered by such items as "Telegrams and Cables," "Wages Account," "General Expense," "Headquarters, Field," "Stationery and Printing," and "Travel and Maintenance." This cost was but a fraction over six per cent. on the cash total. If the estimated money value in field results be taken at three times the cash received and paid, for relief material, food, etc., as stated it will be found that the cost of administration is only about two per cent. In either account or estimate the result is gratifying, though not surprising to the officers of the Red Cross, since the methods pursued are the fruits of a wide experience that evaded no responsibility and learned only to spend wisely for the trust imposed and accepted. It is also satisfactory to know that such expenditures came direct from the "Special Funds" of the Red Cross itself. An examination of the balance sheets accompanying this report shows that of funds expended, the Red Cross is credited with $24,641.93, which leaves an excess for relief over the cost of administration of $17,115.56.

Perhaps this brief financial review of the work achieved may be properly closed by a reference to the sincere enthusiasm and earnestness with which the efforts to raise funds in the United States were animated. The incidents herein mentioned may also illustrate how the wisdom of experience accepts the earnestness and yet discounts without criticism the over confident calculations, to which a noble zeal may run. It would appear that the collection of funds for the purpose of relieving a Christian people in danger of starvation and violent death by knife or bullet—of aiding a historic race in the throes of dissolution from massacre, and dispersion in winter by storm and famine, would be a very easy thing to accomplish. A good many of our countrymen, unaccustomed to great relief work, found the collection of the means needed, a task more than difficult. A single illustration will prove how misleading is the conception. It must be borne in mind always that the Red Cross never solicits funds. It sees its field of benefit work and having fully examined the needs, states them through the press and all other public avenues, to the American people, leaving the response direct to their judgment and generosity. When it is asked to accept the administration of relief funds and material, in fields like this that awaited it in Asia Minor, the trust is surely met, but the Red Cross does not ask for the means and money. Others do that, stating that the work will be under its charge. When it is once accepted there is no retreat, no matter how far the exertions may fall short of reaching the hoped-for results.

Last November (1895), after many petitions had been received and carefully considered, representatives of the great Armenian Relief Committees came to Washington, for the purpose of supplementing such earnest petitions by personal appeals. A conditional consent having been obtained, the subject of funds was brought up by the following question:

"Miss Barton, how much do you think it will cost to relieve the Armenians?"

The question was answered by another: "Gentlemen, you are connected with the various missionary boards, with banks and other great institutions and enterprises. What amount do you consider necessary?"

After deliberation, $5,000,000 was suggested as the proper sum and the question was asked if the Red Cross concurred. Miss Barton, with the faintest suggestion of a smile, replied that she thought $5,000,000 would be sufficient. As the difficulties of raising money became more apparent to the committees, numerous meetings were held and various other amounts suggested, Miss Barton agreeing each time. From $5,000,000 to $500,000, with a guarantee for the balance; then $100,000 cash with $400,000 guaranteed, and so on, until $50,000 was named to start the work with, such sum to be available on the arrival of the Red Cross in Constantinople. The president and a few officers of the Red Cross arrived there on February 15, 1896, but it was late in the following April before the $50,000 was received. These facts as given are intended solely to show the difficulties the committees had to contend with in raising the amount they did.

For general information it will, perhaps, not be inappropriate to state that all relief work is governed and conducted on military lines to preclude the possibility of confusion, as the Red

Cross on fields of disaster is the only organized body in a disorganized community. Thus wherever the organization has control, Miss Barton has personal supervision of all departments: the financial, receiving and disposing of all funds; the correspondence, opening all letters and directing replies; the field, assigning workers to attend to such duties as are best suited to their various abilities, who report daily, if possible, and receive instructions for the prosecution of the work; the supplies, receiving accurate reports of all material and giving directions as to its disposition.

Constantinople, August 1, 1896.   GEORGE H. PULLMAN.

AMERICAN BIBLE HOUSE IN STAMBOUL.

FINANCIAL

OF

RELIEF FUNDS AND

IN ASIA

The American National Red Cross in account

DR.

To The National Relief Committee,	*Ltq.	14,784	51
The New England Relief Committee,	"	5,667	25
The Worcester Relief Committee,	"	402	18
The Ladies' Relief Committee, of Chicago,	"	922	50
The Friends of Phila. through Asa S. Wing,	"	481	69
Citizens of Newark, through C. H. Stout, Esq.,	"	674	65
Citizens of Milton, North Dakota,	"	4	66
St. George's Church S. S., through C. H. Stout, Esq.,	"	40	06
Ransom Post, G. A. R., Wales, Minnesota,	"	2	95
The Davenport, Iowa, Relief Committee,	"	54	78
American Ladies in Geneva, Switzerland,	"	5	85
Miss Phillips, Mission school, Balisori, India,	"	13	20
Mrs. Dr. Galbraith, Terentum, Penn.,	"	3	30
"Sailors' Rest," Genoa, Italy,	"	2	33
A citizen of Chester, New Jersey,	"		02
Miss Mayham Winter, Philadelphia, Penn.,	"	1	14
The American National Red Cross (special),	"	3,376	66
Total,	"	26,437	73

*Ltq. 2,223.78 of this sum was Special Red Cross Funds drawn from Brown Brothers & Company.

BALANCE SHEET

THE

SERVICE OF 1896,

MINOR.

with the Relief Field of Asia Minor.

		CR.
By Telegrams and Cables,	Ltq.	245 12
Cash sent to interior,	"	18,965 70
Relief Expeditions, General,	"	2,917 81
Relief Expeditions, Medical,	"	543 68
Wages Account,	"	421 20
General Expense Account,	"	138 02
Red Cross Headquarters, Field,	"	235 05
Stationery and Printing,	"	128 79
Expense Account, Travel and Maintenance,	"	542 36
Donations for relief of orphan children,	"	100 00
Emergency Fund, deposited with W.W. Peet,	"	2,200 00
Total,		26,437 73

CLARA BARTON, Treasurer.
GEORGE H. PULLMAN, Financial Secretary.
GEO KÜNZEL, Expert Accountant.

I have carefully examined the books, accounts and vouchers of the American National Red Cross, in its relief work in Asia Minor, and find everything correct and accurate. Signed, GEORGE KÜNZEL,
Accountant, Administration
Constantinople, August 1st, 1896. Ottoman Public Debt.

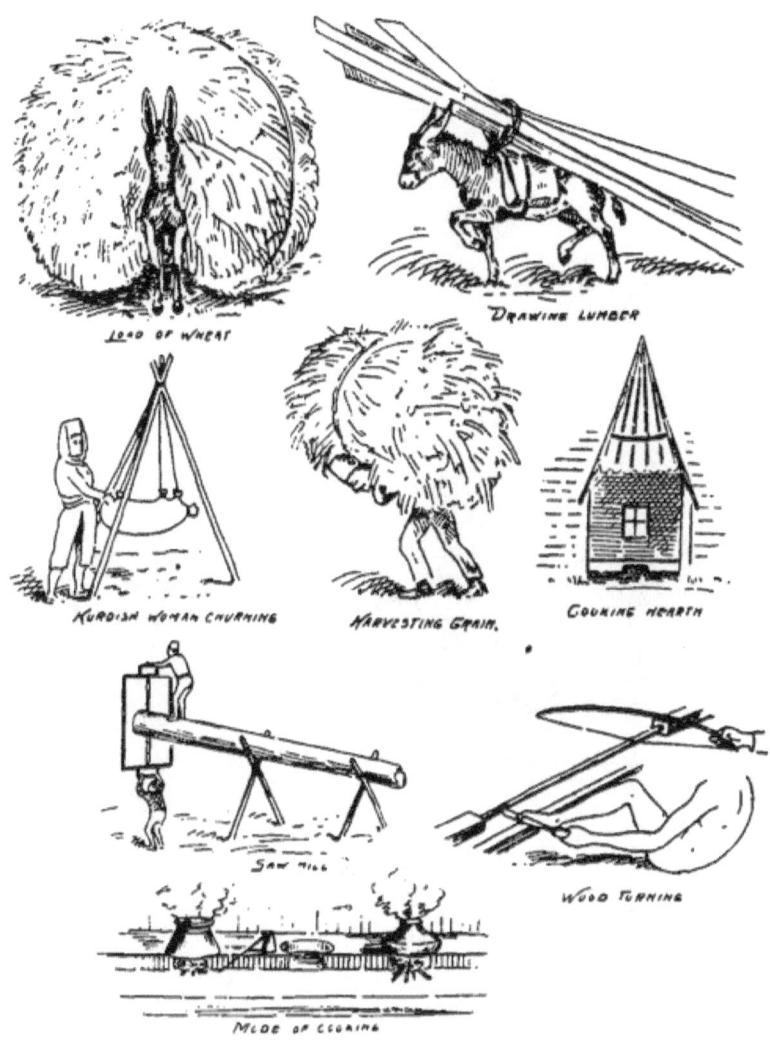

MANNER OF CARRYING BURDENS, METHODS OF WORK, ETC.

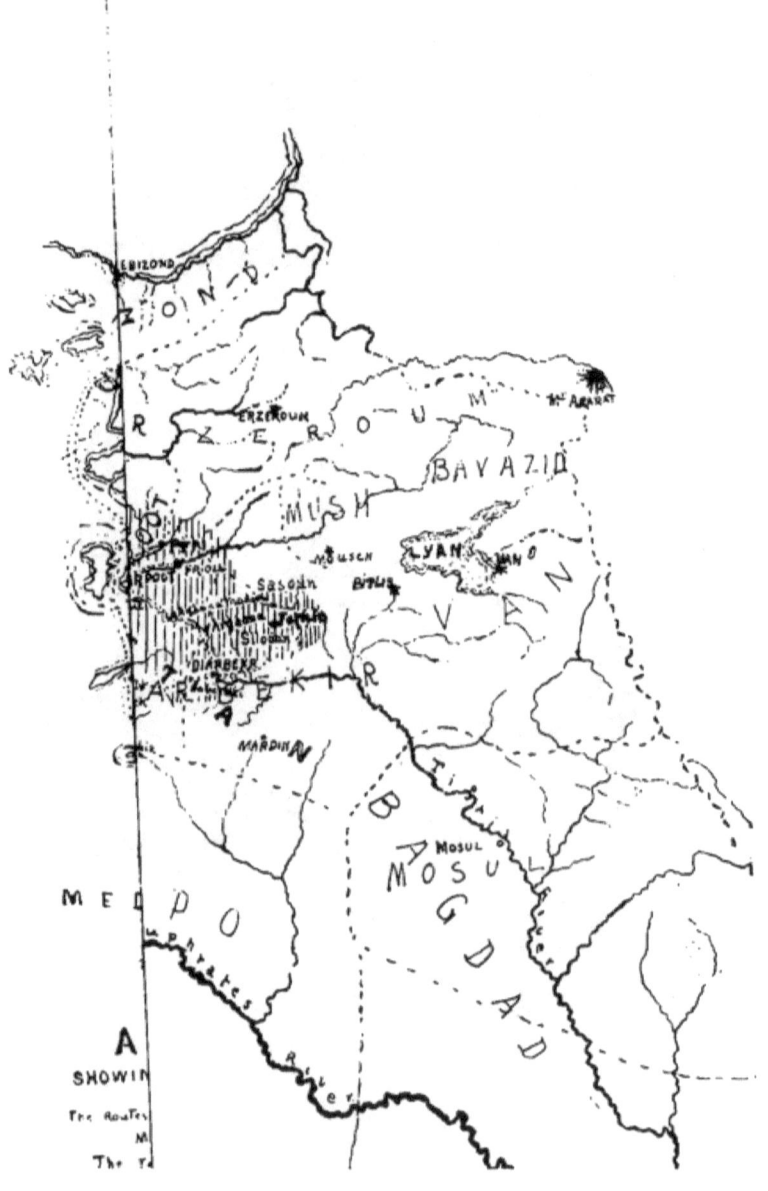

REPORTS

OF

RELIEF FIELD WORK IN ANATOLIA.

J. B. HUBBELL, M. D., General Field Agent.

E. M. WISTAR, Special Field Agent.

C. K. WOOD, Special Field Agent.

IRA HARRIS, M. D., Physician in Charge of Medical Relief in Zeitoun and Marash.

REPORT OF

J. B. HUBBELL, M. D.

GENERAL FIELD AGENT IN CHARGE OF EXPEDITIONS IN THE INTERIOR OF ANATOLIA.

To MISS CLARA BARTON, President:

In speaking of the relief work in Asia Minor, may I be allowed to begin at Constantinople, at which place, while waiting for the necessary official papers for our work, we were all busy selecting and purchasing relief supplies, camping outfit, cooking utensils, and making other preparations for interior travel; and also securing competent interpreters and dragomen. Although the *Irade* of the Sultan granting permission to enter Asia Minor had not yet been received, it naturally fell to me to follow the first shipment of supplies purchased and sent by steamer to the port of Alexandretta as the safest route, to be forwarded again by camels under guard to different places in the interior; and with our own men to follow and attend to the work of distribution. Accordingly, accompanied by interpreter Mason, I left Constantinople on the 10th of March, touching at Smyrna, Latakea, Mersina and Tripoli, reaching Alexandretta on the 18th, and by the kind help of our Consular Agent, Mr. Daniel Walker, and Mr. John Falanga, began making up the caravans for shipment to Aintab, as a central point for the southern field. By the time the caravans were ready and horses for travel selected, Mr. Wistar and Mr. Wood, with dragomen, arrived by steamer from Constantinople. Rev. Dr. Fuller, president of the Aintab (American) College, had also just come through with friends from Aintab to take steamer, himself to return again immediately, and together we all set out under soldier escort the next morning. Alexandretta was in a state of fear while we were there, notwithstanding the fact that the war ships of England, France, Turkey, and the United States lay in her harbor. Kirk Khan, the first stopping place on our journey inland, was threatened with plunder and destruction on the night before our arrival there. At Killis we found the town in a state of fear from the recent massacres. Here, with Dr. Fuller we visited the wounded who were under the good care of a young physician just from the college at Aintab, but without medicine, surgical dressings and appliances. These with other needed things we arranged to send back to him from the supplies that had gone ahead.

Aintab, with its American School, College, Seminary and Hospital buildings standing out in relief and contrast from the native buildings, was a welcome reminder of home; and the greeting of the hundreds of pupils as they came hurrying down the road to welcome back their own loved President, became a welcome for the Red Cross. We were most cordially offered the hospitality of Dr. Fuller's house and home, but as we were still strangers in a strange land, it seemed best to place ourselves in a khan where we could have better opportunity to make an acquaintance with the people to obtain the varied information necessary to accomplish best results in the disposition of our relief. Here we remained long enough to learn the needs of the place and surrounding country, to obtain carefully prepared lists of those artisans needing tools and implements for their various trades and callings. Supplies were left, clothing, new goods for working up, thread, needles, thimbles, medicines, and surgical stores. Aintab is favored with its Mission Hospital; with its surgeon and physician, Dr. Shepard and Dr. Hamilton, and a strong American colony of missionary teachers, besides the Franciscan Brothers, who are doing excellent select work. The Father Superior was killed near Zeitoun. Supplies were selected and made up for Oorfa, Aintab, Marash and other points, while a quantity of supplies, by the kindness of Dr. Fuller, was left in storage in the college building to be forwarded as our inquiries should discover the need. To Oorfa, where the industrial work had been so successfully established by Miss Shattuck, we sent material and implements for working, needles, thread, thimbles, cotton and woolen goods for making up. To Marash and Zeitoun, ready-made goods in addition to new, with surgical appliances and medicines.

From Aintab, Mr. Wood and Mr. Wistar started by way of the most distressed points needing help eastward, and then north to Harpoot; and because of your telegram of the report of typhus and dysentery at Marash and Zeitoun, we started in that direction, with Rev. L. O. Lee, who was returning home. After facing rain, snow and mud for three days we came to Marash. Here we remained until our caravan of goods came on. Typhus, dysentery and small-pox were spreading as a result of the crowded state of the city; Marash had been filled with refugees since the November massacres, notwithstanding a large part of its own dwelling houses had been burned and plundered. The surrounding country had also been pillaged, people killed and villages destroyed, and the frightened remnant of people had crowded in here for protection, and up to this time had feared to return. With insufficient drainage and warm weather coming on, typhus, dysentery and small-pox already in the prisons, an epidemic was becoming general. True, the preachers *requested mothers not to bring children with small-pox* to church, nevertheless the typhus and small-pox spread, and rendered medical supervision a necessity. By the efforts of Mrs. Lee and Mrs. Macallum, wives of the missionaries of the Marash station, a hospital had been established with plenty of patients, but they had no funds for physicians or medicines. Medicines were left and funds furnished for a native doctor educated in America (who himself had just recovered from typhus) and was placed in charge of the hospital and out-of-door service, and was doing efficient work before we left Marash. Arrangements were made with Rev. Mr. Macallum to have tools and implements made and distributed to artisans and villagers; and we left with him to begin this work the sum which you had sent for our own use, 500 liras. By this time Dr. Ira Harris, whom you had called from Tripoli, Syria, with his assistants, arrived for the Zeitoun field. Dr. Harris had his well-filled medical chests and surgical supplies in a mule caravan, and being more needed at other places, we left immediately for Adioman via Besnia, passing through Bazzarjik and Kumaklejercle, a three days' mountain journey. Our officer kindly told us, when we stopped at a Kourdish village for the night, to "order what we want and not pay if we do not want to." But we made it clear to him, that while we are not extravagant in our wants, *we* always pay for what we take. It is customary in this country for villages to entertain soldiers free of charge. At Bazarjik when we inquired concerning the health of the place, an official said they had no sickness *except a few cases of small-pox, and this was confined to children*—that his little girl had it, and she was brought in as a proof.

Besnia was saved from pillage and massacre by the efforts of Pasha Youcab, Osman Zade, Mahund Bey, and several other Turkish Beys, but the surrounding villages were attacked and suffered more or less severely. Some of the women escaped and found protection in Besnia, where they were still living. We did some medical work here and left, in good hands, a moderate sum for emergencies. Our reception by the officials at Besnia, as indeed at every place we have been, large or small, was most cordial and friendly. With only an exception or two, no more considerate treatment could have been expected or asked from any people. Before reaching the city we had heard that there was a feudal war in progress ahead of us, and when the military commander learned that we were intending to go to Adioman, he interposed, saying he could take no responsibility in sending us there; that he had just sent a hundred soldiers out on that road to quell a riot; that it was dangerous, but he would give us a good officer and soldiers for another road to Malatia. This we accepted and four days more of mountain travel, via Paverly, Soorgoo, and Guzena, brought us to the fruit and garden city of Malatia, which formerly had a population of 45,000. It is reported that about 1,500 houses were plundered and 375 were burned, and some thousands of persons killed. The people of all classes were still in fear. A sum of money from friends in America had been received by the missionaries, but its distribution had been delayed several weeks through some formality in the post office, and was but just being made the day we arrived. We left here a sum for special cases and typhus patients, and with a promise to return, pressed on to our objective point, two days' journey more across the Euphrates at Isli to Harpoot, when the limit of our time would be out for meeting the second expedition which arrived only two hours ahead of us. Here the people turned out *en masse* to welcome the Red Cross; the road was lined, the streets and windows filled, and house roofs covered, and all had words of welcome on their lips. We were told by the Rev. Dr. Wheeler, the founder of the Mission and American College of Central Turkey, that we were the second party of Americans, not missionaries, that they had seen in Harpoot in forty years. We were most cordially met by the mission people. Although they, too, had been plundered, and most of their buildings and their homes had gone in the flames, we were offered, most kindly, the shelter of the remaining roofs and seats at their table as long as we would stay. We felt at home again, though startled, too, when we stopped to think we were 8,000 miles away and fifteen days by horseback to the nearest steamer that might start us on a homeward trip or that could carry a letter for us to the outside world. We had been told from the first that Harpoot was suffering more than any other part of the interior, and here we prepared to begin systematic work; Mr. Wistar taking the Char-Sanjak with Peri as a center, the Harpoot plain, and later the Aghan villages. Mr. Wood took the Palou district with two hundred villages, and Silouan in the Vilayet of Diarbekir with one hundred and sixty villages, with the town of Palou and the city of Farkin as centers. While making these arrangements we received your telegram of May 1st: "Typhus and dysentery raging at Arabkir. Can you send doctors with medicines from Harpoot? Please investigate." Upon inquiry we found reported one thousand sick and many dying. This naturally would be my field.

After telegraphing to the various centers for additional medical help without success, we found a native physician, educated in America, Dr. Hintlian, at Harpoot, who was ready to go. Miss Caroline Bush and Miss Seymour of the Mission, with unassumed bravery, volunteered to accompany the expedition. As only one could leave, the choice fell upon Miss Bush. When one reflects that this was a slight little body, never coming up to the majesty of a hundred pounds, with sensitive nature, delicate organization, educated and refined conditions of early life, fears might well be felt for the weight of the lot assumed; but every day's contact convinced us that the springs were of the best of steel, tempered by the glowing fires of experience, thus teaching us how far mind may be superior to matter.

On our first night out, as is frequently the custom in this country, we slept in the stable with our horses—and *smaller animals.* On the second day in crossing the Euphrates at Gabin Madin, the big wooden scoop-shovel ferryboat struck a rock in the swift current mid-stream, and came very near capsizing with its load of luggage, horses and human beings. The boatmen lost their chance of making the opposite shore, and we were in the swift current fast making for the gorge and rapids below. I looked as unconcerned as I could at Miss Bush, only to see that she was as calm as if this was an every-day occurrence or that she had been from childhood accustomed to such experiences. We knew she had not, only she had lived long enough in the interior not to be frightened at anything that might happen. However, another rock was reached near the bluff and we unloaded. Each leading his horse and the pack animals following, we climbed up over the edge of a precipice, over loose stones, slippery earth and ragged rocks, back to the landing we should have made had we gone directly across. Our next day's travel was through a cold, pouring rain, into the ruined city of Arabkir, but notwithstanding the rain, hundreds of people stood in the streets as we passed to make their "salaams" and to say their word of welcome to those who had come to bring the gifts of another land to the suffering, the sick and needy of their own. Passing through the rain, we arrived at the native pastor's house, which had been saved by a Turkish military officer and cleared of refugees and typhus patients for our installation.

Nearly the entire city of Arabkir was in ruins; only heaps of stones where houses had been. Out of 1,800 homes but few remained; the markets as well as the dwellings were destroyed, and the people, plundered and destitute, were crowded into the few remaining houses, down with the typhus. We were told that six hundred had already died of the disease, and the people's physician, the only one in that part of the country, was in prison. Later, we were told that the arrival of help changed the character of the disease the moment it was known that we had come. Miss Bush went with us directly into the sick-rooms, and the presence of a woman gave cheer and strength. A hundred patients were seen daily. After the first wants of the typhus patients had been met, the long neglected surgical cases were looked after, and many lives and limbs were saved. The medical and surgical efforts gave gratifying results, of which Dr. Hintlian will make a special report from his daily record.

Immediately upon our arrival, the Gregorian Church and school buildings which escaped destruction, were offered for our use as a hospital. These rooms were admirably adapted for this purpose, but by selecting and employing persons already in need of help as assistants and nurses, we found that we could better care for the sick in their own quarters than to attempt to remove them to a hospital, where the congregation of sick would only be increased. To give employment was the *one* thing needed for the well, therefore we made no hospitals but employed competent, healthy women in need, instructed and put them to care for sick families, also in need but of another kind. The piaster a woman earned for a day's work gave food for herself and for her own family, and gave the sick family the services necessary to save their lives. The necessary beds for the patients were furnished.

A sheep or a goat given where there was a helpless babe or mother would give food for both, and be a permanent property that would grow by the increase of its own young. A small sum for fowls would be a gift that would furnish more than its value in eggs for food for present use. It would prove a small investment that must multiply in kind and value as chicks were hatched. While medical work was going on other forms of relief were also in progress. A supply of tools had been ordered from Harpoot directly upon our arrival, for blacksmiths, carpenters, tinkers, masons, stone workers, etc. The blacksmiths were set to work making sickles for cutting grass and reaping grain, shovels, plows, and other implements for farmers. Others were put at making spinning-wheels for the destitute women, who with these could earn their own living; others made weaving looms. Out of the 1,200 hand looms formerly in the city it was said only forty remained. Arabkir was the chief manufacturing center for native cotton cloth, and if a man had a loom which would cost three medjidieh (about $2.50) he could earn his own family's living. Field and garden seeds were bought in quantity and distributed. For the villages which had no cattle we gave oxen for plowing the fields. Sometimes with the oxen, cows were given, with instructions that in this stress of need the cows should be made to work with the oxen, even while they were giving milk for the family. Thus they would secure a double service for one outlay. Melkon Miranshabian, the druggist, kindly offered his services, and we arranged with him to take up special cases and to continue to care for them after we would no longer be able to remain on the field. Then, feeling that we might safely leave this work in the hands of Dr. Hintlian, we went to Egin to arrange for distribution in the Aghan villages, Miss Bush accompanying.

The inquiry will naturally be made as to how relief was received. The gratitude of the people was almost overwhelming at times. If you could

MARASH.

A TURKISH VILLAGE.

SINNAMOD, SUBURB OF HARPOOT.

A ZAPTIEH.

A WRECK.

A KHAN.

DR. HUBBELL AND GUARD.

only have heard the blessings that were poured out upon you, the Red Cross, and the good people everywhere who have aided, you would realize that deep as the need, so fervent and sincere have been the thankful prayers and blessings that the unfortunate people who survive the massacre could alone render to all who help them. To you and your name especially were they responsive. Of all this, I would say we often had most gratifying evidence and expression on the lonely roads, in the stricken homes, and through personal letters from many sources.

When we were some six miles out on the road to Egin, we met the leading men of the village of Shepik coming to town; they had heard that we were going away soon, and the villagers had sent this committee to Arabkir to express their gratitude for what they had received and for all that had been done for them. This was five or six weeks after we had made a distribution of seeds, and as we came in sight of their village we saw gardens green with onions, potatoes, beans, cucumbers, melons, squash, pumpkins, etc., from the seeds we had given. Here too, the women were in the fields cutting the grass and grain with the sickles which the blacksmiths had made from the iron and steel we had furnished. The men were plowing with the plows and oxen we had supplied and, notwithstanding they had been plundered of every movable thing and their houses burned or destroyed, there was an air of prosperity in the fields that banished thoughts of want or suffering. We rode on past the little room where the school was kept and every child rose to his feet and made a most profound, though youthful bow to our passing company.

Egin is an old, strangely beautiful city, inhabited by the descendants of the noble families of Mosul (NINEVEH) who fled to this mountain stronghold on the Euphrates during the Persian invasion, many years ago, and they are still a royal and gentle people. At Egin the officials declared it unsafe for us to go to the villages as we had proposed. Accordingly we made purchases in this market and sent them to the needy points. Egin had bought the Kourds off with 1,500 liras, and consequently it had remained up to the date of our arrival unharmed through all the destruction about it. We also left a sum of money with a responsible committee for eight unfortunate villages, and did what medical work we could in our short stay. We then returned to Harpoot.

On our road back, Miss Bush had with her a young girl whom we were taking to Harpoot for safety (we had frequent charges of this kind), and she wanted me to stop at her favorite beautiful village of Bervan, for a pleasant picture to carry back in memory to America. We had a long day's journey at best to reach our village, and had met with delays; four hours in the morning waiting for a zaptieh. Our muleteer left us at the ferry some twelve miles back, in order to stop over night at his own village;

and the second zaptieh was two hours late, but having started we must keep on through the mountain pass, and it was ten o'clock at night when we reached the village. Our zaptieh took us to the house of the "Village-man" (each village is provided with such a personage whose duty it is to see that shelter is provided for travellers). We rode up together and the zaptieh pounded on the door. The dog on the roof barked viciously, then all the dogs in the village barked. A woman on another roof above this one raised herself and talked, then shouted down the chimney-hole (the roof is the sleeping place in warm weather), after a time she pointed with her hand and the zaptieh started off in the direction indicated; the moon had gone down and it was too dark to see anything distinctly. He came to a small pile, poked it with his foot, punched it with his gun, kicked it. After a time a part of the pile raised itself in a sort of surprised astonishment, mystified, uncertain, complicated attitude—evidently looking at the "poker." Then the pile expressed itself emphatically, the zaptieh did the same more emphatically, each in turn louder and louder, all with necessary and unnecessary gesticulation. Then the pile got up and began on our servants for having the pack mules and animals on his roof. After these had been led off the house, he wanted to know what we came there for anyway, at that time of night, to wake him up when there were six other villages we could have gone to; why didn't we go to one of them? Then our zaptieh changed his tone and attitude and in the most polite, persuasive, pleading voice and manner, tried to explain that he himself was not to blame for all this trouble, he was under orders and had to come with these people; he couldn't help doing his duty. But this made no impression, and we were told there was no place for us. None could be found at this time of night; besides there was no barley for the horses, and nothing was to be done unless it was to go on and try another village. Our zaptiah seemed to have exhausted his resources and said no more. Other villagers had come and were standing around the "village-man," who still insisted that he could do nothing. Miss Bush quietly suggested "*Argentum.*" We got down from our horse, went around carelessly, and slipped a "cherek" (a five piaster piece) into his fingers. He took and felt of it, and then went away without a word. After about ten minutes he returned with a light, a door was opened close beside us, and we unloaded our animals, put them all in, took in the luggage, went in ourselves, got our supper, spread our blankets, drove away our audience of villagers, fastened the stable door and announced to ourselves that we were one hour into the "next day," and went to sleep. We were off again the next morning before the sun was up. This is a sample incident of what happened in frequent variation during interior travel.

At Harpoot we arranged for supplying tools and cattle to the remaining villages which we failed to reach from Egin. Here, too, we found Mr. Wistar busy supplying harvesting and threshing implements, and cattle for plowing in the Harpoot plain and villages. In this vilayet there are upwards of two hundred villages either plundered or wholly destroyed, and from these many persons of all classes came for medical or surgical help.

Preparations were made to work in Malatia, where, some weeks before, we had ordered supplies and medicines sent to be ready for our arrival, but owing to the unsettled conditions there, no such work could be done to advantage. The time for our return to Constantinople was drawing near and on the 27th of June we were ready to start for the Black Sea. We called to pay our respects to the Governor of Harpoot and found him as cordial as he had always been. Inquiries were made and explanations given, so that he might more thoroughly understand the character and purposes of the Red Cross. His Excellency remarked that it gave to those engaged in the work great opportunities to become acquainted with different countries, and that we must have found Turkey the most difficult of them all to work in. He regretted that he himself had been of so little assistance to our efforts, etc., but we took pleasure in saying that he had done at all times all that we had asked and ofttimes more. Speaking for those associated with our work I could safely say that all the recollections of our personal relations with the vali of Harpoot will remain with us as pleasant and satisfactory.

The principal food and the main crop of the interior is wheat, and this year's growth wherever we have been is reported to be unusually good. If the wheat can be distributed where the destitution will be this coming winter, many lives may be saved; if not, many must inevitably be lost for want of food. When we left the Harpoot valley harvesting had well begun, and was even more briskly going on as we neared the Euphrates, which we crossed for the last time at Isli on the 29th of June. The usual Euphrates ferry-boat is twenty-four to thirty feet long, eight feet wide, and two feet high at one end and eight at the other where a rudder, or sweep, forty feet long is hung. An American frequently sees methods of work and management that lead him sometimes, when *first* traveling, to make suggestions. After seeing the ferrymen upon many occasions putting loaded wagons on the boat, lifting them by main force some two or three feet with much awkwardness over the edge of the craft, we ventured to suggest that two planks laid on the bank and end of the boat so as to roll the wagons in or out would save much trouble and time and extra help and labor. We were met with this unanswerable reply: "Who would pay for them?"

To Malatia we carried money to the people from their relatives in America which had been intrusted to Dr. Barnum at Harpoot. We also left in the hands of a responsible committee a fund for artisans' tools, and a smaller sum for food and supplies in special needy cases. The state of prosperity and feeling of security in Malatia was not nearly so propitious as in Harpoot. We saw few people here, nor could we remain long enough to attempt the relief work that was probably more needed than in many other districts. The accompanying letter received since our return to the United States, from the Rev. Dr. Gates, president of the Harpoot American College, gives, as will be seen on reading, a most interesting account of the work done and the money distributed after our departure by himself and Miss Bush:

HARPOOT, TURKEY, Aug. 19, 1896.

MISS CLARA BARTON:

Dear Friend: Having recently received a telegram from Dr. Hubbell saying that the balance of funds left in our hands might be used as I suggested in a letter to him, that is, for Chemisligusek and Malatia regions, Miss Bush, Prof. Teuikejian and I, accompanied by Mrs. Harris, went to Malatia July 31st, and remained there two weeks. The time was most opportune. The Reform Commissioner, Marshall Shakir Pasha, had just arrived in Malatia and our English Vice Consul, Mr. Fontana, had gone on to meet him, so we were able to avail ourselves of their presence in our efforts to start business and set the people on their feet.

Malatia depends largely on trade with the Kourdish villages. It is the centre of trade for some 250 of these. The Christian population go to them for business. Some sow grain, others do carpenter work, shoemaking and the like. A very large proportion of the Christian population have their business in the villages. Since the events of last November all intercourse has been stopped because of the hostile attitude of these villagers towards Christians. Hence artisans and tradesmen were idle and in danger of losing all means of employment.

I at once applied myself to induce the government to insure protection to Christians in going to the villages and collecting their dues. The consul worked splendidly on this and other lines. The government issued a strong proclamation to the Kourdish Agbas, the local governor called them, and placed them under bonds to keep the peace, and before we left the artisans had begun to go out to the villages.

Then we made careful lists of the people according to their trades and occupations, and gave them aid to use in purchasing tools and starting themselves in work by which to earn their own living.

We found 1883 orphans and 630 widows. The widows we supplied with spinning wheels by which they can earn something. though not enough t) support a family. Mrs. Harris has taken samples of embroideries for which she hopes to find a market in Europe. This will be a great help to women if successful.

Of houses there were 567 burned, and the people are now living in the gardens, but the Armenian Relief Committee in Constantinople has given funds to aid in rebuilding, and soon houses will go up all over the city.

Artisans have been supplied with tools, and they can now go to the villages and use them, and to one village we gave twenty-three oxen with which to gather their harvest and sow for another year.

A better state of feeling has begun to be manifested between Turks and Christians. Eleven prisoners were released, and the people spoke with joy and gratitude of their improved condition. We have received several touching letters of thanks from them.

I hope and trust this visit will go far towards relieving the distress in that city, though some will need help this coming winter. There will be great need of bedding and clothing when cold weather sets in, not only in Malatia but in many other places. With sincere thanks for your aid,

I remain yours truly,

C. F. GATES.

The sun is extremely hot during the interior summer season, hence, when the moon was favorable we traveled by night, leaving the saddle long enough to sleep in the "Araba," (a sort of small, springless, covered wagon used where there are roads) so as to have the day to work in while our horses rested. When we could do so in our journey we left funds for specified purposes, but frequently the sufferers felt safer without such assistance and declined to receive it. At Sivas we gave a fund for farmers' tools. Here the grain crop was later than in the valleys further south. We also left here with the Rev. Messrs. Perry and Hubbard, a horse, in order to facilitate their relief work. From Malatia several families and individuals placed themselves under the protection of the Red Cross and its guards in order to go in safety to the coast. A portion of this road is infested with brigands and a strong guard is necessary, in fact it is needed throughout the whole region. The Government took particular care of us by giving us a brigand as a special guard through the dangerous part of the road, saying that we should be safer with him than with the regular military guard. A few weeks before a rich caravan was robbed on this road, and when we passed we had the interesting pleasure of taking tea and journeying for a while with the chief of these brigands who had two days before been enlisted in Government service. With the ample Government protection we have at all times had, we seldom felt concern for our personal safety, notwithstanding that in places where we visited there was often a great deal of anxiety and fear on the part of the people for their own safety and that of their friends, or their property if they had any.

Tokat and Amasia were on our homeward route—the latter place being the site of the ancient castle of Mithridates, King of Pontus.

At Samsoun we had two saddle-horses to dispose of, and our Consular Agent, Mr. Stephapopale, having a stable, kindly offered to sell them to the best profit for us, and to see that the proceeds were used in aiding the refugees who crowd to the coast in the hope of getting farther on, but only find themselves stranded and unable to return, becoming thereby veritable sufferers.

On the 16th of July we reached the Bosphorus, four months and six days from the time we started out from Constantinople for the interior, glad of the privilege and power we have enjoyed as messengers to carry some of the gifts that have been entrusted to your care by the people of the world, for the innocent, unfortunate sufferers of Anatolia.

Wherever we have met the Missionaries, Protestant or Catholic, we have found them devoting most, if not all, of their time to the work of relieving the suffering about them, regardless of sect or nationality; but in all cases their fields of work have been greater than their strength or their means. With them we have worked always harmoniously and without consciousness of difference of place or creed; and to them and to many others we are indebted for courtesies and for hospitalities that will always be remembered with gratitude.

The real work of the relief expedition was greatly aided by the hearty co-operation of every European and American resident with whom we came in contact. Each did all in his power for our aid. At Alexandretta, for every courtesy and assistance. we are indebted to our U. S. Consular agent, Mr. Daniel Walker, and likewise to his business agent, Mr. John Falanga, in the forwarding of our supplies and caravans to the interior.

Rev. Dr. Fuller, president of Central Turkey Armenian College, together with his brave, practical, accomplished wife, who gave us much information and arranged for us in the college buildings a warehouse and shipping station for goods and supplies. To the Franciscan brothers, also of Aintab, we are indebted for aid and courtesies. Here also, we had the good fortune to meet the English Vice Consul Fitzmaurice, whose recently acquired knowledge of the country and conditions, gained from his official travels in the distressed districts, was cordially given and most gratefully received.

At Marash we shall long remember with gratitude the brave people in the American and European missions, nearly all of whom lost property and friends in the general disturbance (massacre). Especially do we remember Rev. and Mrs. Macallum, Rev. and Mrs. L. O. Lee, Miss Hess and Miss Blakley. We are particularly indebted to the Italian Consul just from Zeitoun and making a temporary stop in Marash, for courtesies and information, and likewise to the Catholic Archbishop Monsignor Avadian Curkian and the Franciscan Brothers of Marash, each and all for courtesies on the lines of our work. Many others here also we remember with gratitude, but space forbids our attempting to name all. At Bazarjik, Ahemet Zade Mahomet Bey, and at Malatia, to Aziz Zada Mustafa Aga, to each for great courtesies and hospitalities.

Harpoot American Mission became our home in every sense of the American word, while we were in Central Turkey, notwithstanding the fact that nearly all its property and buildings had been lost by plunder and fire.

Rev. C. F. Gates, D. D., President of the American Mission College, a genial scholar and practical business man, possessing a wide knowledge of the country, the people and conditions, made his counsels of greatest service as so large a part of our work was performed in this section. He was our banker and advisor. Rev. Dr. H. A. and Mrs. Barnum's home was ours every day that we were there.

Miss C. E. Bush, earnest, experienced, cultivated and refined, who joined our expedition and remained through the Arabkir typhus epidemic, and later went with us to Egin, we shall ever remember with gratitude for her help and cheer among the disconsolate sick and suffering.

The English Vice Consul, R. A. Fontana, proved an untiring friend, genial and ready at all times to assist officially and personally.

To the Franciscan Brothers we are indebted for hospitalities. To Dr. H. Hintlian, whose successful work among the sick, both at Arabkir and at Harpoot, made his service felt, so are we grateful.

In Arabkir we are indebted to Bodville Bedrose, whose home was ours while we remained in our work there; no less for his ever cheerful and ready help in every emergency or delicate undertaking. The Protestant, Gregorian, Catholic and Turkish friends, too many to name, we remember with friendship and gratitude for their many deeds of kindness.

At Egin we will ever remember the generous hospitality during our short stay with the families of Nicoghos Agha Jangochyan and Alexander Effendi Kasabyan, noblemen, who by their energy and liberality saved the city and people from destruction, while the country around about was being plundered and burned, and who gave us great assistance in furnishing tools and implements to this section of the country.*

Rev. and Mrs. Perry, Rev. A. B. and Mrs. Hubbard, and Messrs. Brewer, of Sivas, we hold in grateful remembrance for hospitalities and

---

*NOTE. Since we left Egin we learn that these gentlemen with nearly two thousand others have been killed. These families were the center of a large community, among the most charming and cultivated people we were privileged to meet during our absence from home.

their cheerful acceptance of the task imposed in the distribution of additional agricultural tools and implements for this district.

To Dr. Milo A. Jewett, our Consul, and to Major Bullman, the English Consul, we are indebted for courtesies and hospitalities, and to our Consular Agent at Samsoun for kind relief services in the furtherance of our work.

To the Turkish officials everywhere we are grateful for their careful supervision of our personal safety, and for the general personal freedom allowed ourselves wherever we worked. To the officers and guards who always accompanied us in our journeys through cold and heat, on the road by night or day, over desolate plain or mountain trail, for bringing us

RED CROSS EXPEDITIONS PASSING THROUGH THE VALLEY OF CATCH BEARD.

safely through from sea to sea without a scratch or harm of any kind, for all this we are most assuredly grateful, and oft recall the cheerful vigilant service and special courtesies we enjoyed at their hands which could only be prompted by the most friendly feelings and consideration.

But we do not forget, dear Miss Barton, that the success of this expedition is due to your careful and constant oversight and direction of all our movements, from the seat of government at Constantinople, from first to last, and to the conviction which you had impressed upon the Sublime Porte of your own and your officers' honesty, integrity and singleness of purpose. Hence for your statesmanship and generalship and constant oversight, we would express our warmest gratitude.

MISS CAROLINE E. BUSH.

FIRST EXPEDITION EMBARKING ON FERRYBOAT, EUPHRATES RIVER.

REV. H. N. BARNUM, D. D.

REV. C. F. GATES, D. D.

We are grateful for the gratitude of the people we tried to relieve. It was universal and sincere. The kindness with which we were everywhere welcomed, and the assistance so cordially rendered by all the noble men and women with whom it has been my good fortune to become personally acquainted. Surrounded as they were with desolation, dangers and misery, they will be remembered for their worth and devotion to duty.

Constantinople, August 1, 1896. J. B. HUBBELL.

SUB-REPORT OF DR. HINTLIAN.

To J. B. HUBBELL, M. D., GENERAL FIELD AGENT:

In reply to your request for a report of the medical work in connection with the relief of Arabkir and Harpoot, I hand a list of the patients treated and the following summary:

Typhus in Arabkir,	966
Typhus in Amberga (suburb),	29
Cases of malarial fever,	41
General diseases,	205
Eye cases,	178
Surgical cases,	25
Skin diseases,	65
Typhus cases in Todem	50
Typhus cases and general diseases in Harpoot,	63
Partial paralysis,	8
	1,611
Deaths from typhus,	9
Death from chronic pleurisy,	1
	10

Nine deaths out of nine hundred cases gives less than one per cent. of mortality among the typhus patients under our care in Arabkir, where before we began our treatment the mortality had been twenty-six per cent.

Our treatment of the typhus cases was simple as you know. First, to ventilate the room; second, to furnish a bed or beds where there were none and this was a frequent symptom; third, when the entire family was down or when the sick were without proper attention, to furnish a person to take the cases until recovery; and fourth, to see that food of a proper kind was on hand, and our prescription cards frequently read: "Bed, one bushel of wheat, or —— piasters for broth, —— drops of hydrochloric acid, for drink.

During our medical work in Arabkir from May 13 to June 23, we kept a record of cases treated, together with the treatment used. In this time we either treated or gave treatment to 1561 patients. Of these 966 were typhus cases out of which we lost nine by death. From the best sources of information we could reach we learned that about 500 had died of this disease before we arrived. The remaining 586 cases were of general disease, surgical, chronic, ordinary fever, &c. Out of this number we lost one case by death. In our medical work here we met with quite a number of cases, as elsewhere, of semi-paralysis brought on by fright or fear. These yielded under mild treatment, and before we came away nearly all these cases gave promise for a complete recovery in a short time.

Most of the surgical cases were gunshot or other wounds that had been without treatment since last November. The conditions were often deplorable but they responded marvelously to our treatment.

A peculiar disease of the skin had been frequently observed. The symptoms were excessive nervous itching, sometimes with eruptions. It seemed to be the result of excessive fear. These cases usually required, in addition to the treatment of similar skin diseases, some nerve tonic in order to obtain most satisfactory results.

The typhus in this country is an eruptive fever, induced by unhygienic conditions, as living in over-crowded rooms without ventilation, and using impure water. It spreads by contagion; while it proves fatal in a large degree when neglected, we have found it to yield readily to simple treatment and good nursing combined with fresh air. My medication has been usually but little more than acid drinks.

I have not attempted to make a detailed report nor to enumerate the most distressing condition of these suffering people, but merely to give results of my work.

Before leaving the city of Arabkir the druggist, Melkon Miranshahian, who was the first ready to assist, joined in our work during the last days there, and made himself familiar with the surgical and other cases and with our methods of treatment, for the purpose of continuing the work of relief himself as a Red Cross worker as long as his services might be needed after we left.

You know better than I can repeat it the good work done in this city and villages—no less among the well than among the sick—and as you also know, among every race and sect of people needing help. But their unbounded gratitude, their blessings on you and Miss Barton, the Red Cross, and the American people, spoken in strange tongues, it is my privilege to know better than you, and I too, am deeply grateful for the privilege and the honor of working with the Red Cross, and shall always remain   Yours most truly,   HAGOP HINTLIAN.

Harpoot, August 20, 1896.

REPORT OF

EDWARD M. WISTAR,

OF PHILADELPHIA, SPECIAL FIELD AGENT, IN CHARGE OF

SECOND EXPEDITION.

To Miss CLARA BARTON, President:

Upon my return from the field of active work in Asia Minor, you have asked for a summary of my report made to you from time to time. It follows herewith:

Perhaps it was the 9th of December last, that upon looking over my office mail, there met my eye a letter from you and Mr. Pullman. Suffering in Turkey had been much on my mind during the previous few days, and before opening your envelope there seemed to come to me the thought, "What if this prove a call for services in Armenia?" Your kind preliminaries were followed by the query, "If we find it possible to go to Armenia will it be possible for you to go with us?" After full deliberation I wired you that I would be at your service, and immediately made arrangements for leaving home. Subsequent correspondence and an interview with you in Washington placed me in an attitude of readiness. Later (the 22d of January having been fixed for leaving America), I was expecting to accompany you, when for certain good reasons a wire received about noon of the 21st said, "Not to-morrow, wait for further advice." This advice finally came by cable from Constantinople on the 19th of February, "come Saturday (22d), and bring another man." Accordingly Mr. Charles King Wood sailed with me on the following day, the 22d. We were in London within the week and welcomed by you in your own home in Constantinople on the 7th of March.

The important matter of selecting and contracting with a suitable interpreter, and other preliminary arrangements, detained us a few days in Constantinople, but these being made and *teskeres* (traveling passports) granted by the authorities, we took passage for Alexandretta, in Syria, at the northeast corner of the Mediterranean. The passage was circuitous and long stops were made for cargo so that eight days were spent on the voyage, but we were cheered upon our arrival to find Dr. Hubbell in Alexandretta, where he had been getting off a large caravan. That afternoon all our *teskeres* were *viséd* for Aintab and at [sunrise the next day the journey into the interior was commenced. Passing over the broad plains of Antioch and by Hymmum-Khan we reached Killis in three days, shortly after the massacre there. An irresponsible mob followed and jeered at us as we entered the town, but offered no actual violence. It may be said here that during all our stay in the country the *saptiehs*, or guards deputed for our personal escorts, were always respectful, and, so far as appeared, vigilant in their care of us. At one place I recall hearing an officer instruct the guard that if anyone attempted to interfere with the Americans he should be summarily dealt with.

At Killis we called first on the Kaimikam, the head of the local government, who received us cordially, and indeed in all subsequent visits made to the authorities we were always courteously treated. After two days investigation it did not seem best to open a campaign of relief here as your caravan of supplies had already gone to Aintab and to which place we were all *viséd*.

Reaching this latter place we arranged for the distribution of your goods and also some clothing. etc., contributed by the Friends' Mission of Constantinople. Finding relief work being done here and feeling the greater need of points yet beyond, it was decided to separate, going by different routes so as to touch as many such places as possible, and to meet again at Harpoot if it should prove practicable. Leaving Dr. Hubbell, with Mr. Wood still accompanying me, I set out for Oorfa on the 6th of April, passing through Nisib and many smaller mud hut villages, crossed the swollen Euphrates and reached Beredjik the second day and Oorfa in two more. The world knows of the heroic work of Miss Corinna Shattuck; how she was alone in Oorfa during the dark days of December 28th and 29th; how she saved in her own house scores of terrified refugees; and how she is still laboring or striving in her quiet, unobtrusive way to relieve the needs of those about her. It is not necessary that I say more—her name is one that should be remembered among the heroines of Christian womanhood with a lustre undimmed to the last. It was a great privilege to be able to offer her sympathy and encouragement.

About $900, or in exact figures, 200 Turkish liras ($4.40), were expended in co-operation with Miss Shattuck, and during twelve days spent at Oorfa arrangements for the making of a considerable supply of household utensils were effected. This operation commended itself as giving employment to a considerable number of efficient workmen, who were found destitute and because the product gave relief to a large number of destitute people which should be permanent in character.

At dawn, the 21st of April, we were again in the saddle following the trail towards the city of Diarbekir ; passing through Severek, two days' en route from Oorfa, a town and district badly plundered but which had received some help from Oorfa, and to which more funds were sent later, we reached the ancient walled city on the forenoon of the 24th.

At Diarbekir we were most hospitably entertained by Mr. Hallward, the British Consul, spending Saturday and Sunday there to give our horses a needed rest, to gather information and to report to you, as you may remember, and thence over the Taurus Mountains to Harpoot. Rev. Dr. H. N. Barnum, the veteran missionary, Dr. C. F. Gates, president of the Mission College, other missionaries and a host of the inhabitants greeted our arrival at the entrance of the city, and we were assigned comfortable quarters in one of the Mission houses. To us, strangers and travel-worn as we were, it seemed almost more than an incident, when with no other previous arrangement, except that upon parting at Aintab it was proposed that we meet again at Harpoot, and with no possible communication between us in more than three weeks, we saw Dr. Hubbell with his expedition enter the city from Malatia, later the same day. We felt our way for a day or two and then with fresh advice from you set to work to arrange details for active personal service in different sections of the Harpoot field, gaining as much information as possible relative to requirements and conditions. Incidentally, but with direct purpose, a number of villages were visited and interviews had with recommended men from different localities. Mr. Wood now arranged with Dr. Hubbell for funds and work apart from me. My first call, before commencing the work of the great Harpoot plain, was from Char-Sandjak, with Peri as a center, a district lying northeast from Harpoot, about two days' distant across a rugged mountainous country and two branches of the Euphrates, with a population of about 8,500 persons, inhabiting 74 villages, all but four of which had been wholly or in large part plundered during the disturbances of last autumn. Here as in other places visited, there was an urgent need of clothing, food and bedding ; for tools and farming implements and a little capital for starting industries; also for seed. Accompanied by my interpreter I was able to work early and late for three weeks in this district and with gratifying results. Native cloth from hand-looms was bought from anyone who had it to sell at a fixed price. It was immediately cut into garments which were given out to be sewed by the women in their homes and returned the following morning ; these suits were often clothing the nakedness of the people on that day. Thus the one outlay was made to serve three different purposes—a market for the weavers' cloth, work for hundreds of women, and clothing for the most needy. About 150 artisans in need of tools and small capital were reinstated in business. Two hundred oxen and five hundred implements and tools, including a large proportion of plows were bought and distributed; bread rations were given out daily.

At the end of three weeks a walk through the bazaars of Peri showed a large increase in activity in the shops, particularly of the blacksmiths, coppersmiths and shoemakers, and the general condition of trade was much improved.

The field was left in the hands of a good native committee, with some supplies, afterwards much increased when visited by me. Returning to Harpoot I engaged in further relief work there, looking towards the giving of work-animals and tools, and the re-establishment of industries. Our particular efforts were to save the great grain crop of the Harpoot plain, which for weeks past had been developing before our eyes and was now beginning to turn from green to gold—the one bar, as appeared, against famine in the future. In the many perplexing issues always at hand there was the greatest need to stand one's ground firmly in this purpose, for if the grain crop could not be properly harvested and secured the number of ragged and starving would be wofully augmented and so lie again for the coming winter on the hearts of the charitable world.

During these months it was necessary that the work be as rapid and continuous as possible. Headquarters were in succession at Harpoot, at Peri, on the road, and again at Harpoot. All one's previous experiences were in requisition. Committees of investigation were sought out and arranged and reports and petitions from towns and villages and from scores of individuals were received daily. Bargains for grain, cattle, cloth, tools and a variety of them, and of other merchandise were negotiated, reports were filed, and wants and agreements noted.

As my own cashier the responsibility thickened, all transactions, the largest as well as the least, having to be met in ready coin carried in belt pockets and saddle bags. President Gates, of Euphrates College at Harpoot, acted as our general banker, and in this as in other ways his good judgment and sagacity were of the greatest assistance. All payments were made personally and a complete cash account, tendered you with this, was kept.

Applicants of course flocked by hundreds and finally by thousands, the great mass of them on foot. Many had to return disappointed as before indicated.

Nearly all the grain was distributed under my personal supervision by a small committee of native men. Where this was not feasible I issued orders to heads of families, having first secured an option on a good supply at a fixed price.

Tools and implements were contracted for according to sample and at a stated price; or at times I informed the blacksmiths at Harpoot or other towns that cash would be paid for all delivered during certain days at a standard rate, if properly branded. Being firm in this position from the outset, efforts to deceive me and defraud those for whom the work was being done were avoided.

These articles were in large part distributed village by village, and gathering knowledge by experience gained in other fields of relief and acting under your distinct orders and well-tried policy, the people were supplied direct, or through a village committee appointed by themselves, and always vouched for under the systematic investigation your method required. They came from all parts of the section. Your instructions provided for the appointment of a general or district advisory and investigating committee, made up of a small number of leading native merchants, pastors, and others as thoroughly conversant with local wants and individual characters. They received or had referred to them all the local applications for relief. This committee required due reports, submitting the results to me, and I took such action as my best judgment and knowledge would admit of. Clothing and bedding were thus distributed from my quarters by reliable men who knew the people. All those who received money were interviewed, carefully examined and paid by myself, as it was frequently the case that the needy individuals could do better for themselves than I could do for them, by having a small sum given them. Most cattle and pack animals were purchased by individuals for themselves or by a small committee for certain residents of a given village. In such cases I carefully used ordinary business precautions to secure trustworthy results, and required reports. Animals and tools were branded as directed by you. This occasioned some difficulty when dealing with a fresh set of people but they finally came to appreciate its usefulness as a matter of safety and gave assistance when required.

It was our purpose to lift the people up from their deplorable ruins, and to encourage them to look toward reassuring normal conditions, using therein whatever I could command to bring this about.

The estimated result of our work in Harpoot city and district with its 85 villages, was the re-establishment of 4,575 artisans, the providing of 700 oxen, cows, asses and horses; nearly 3,000 farm implements and other tools were made and distributed, as also 3,500 articles of clothing, 500 beds and 1,470 bushels of grain. Medicine was also furnished to fever patients.

I remained in Harpoot with this work until the third of July, when having received your recall, Mr. Wood was summoned from Farkin and so returned together to Constantinople, via Sivas, Samsoun and the Black Sea, arriving at Constantinople on the 20th of July.

REPORT OF MR. WISTAR.

The guidance and support of the Unseen Hand has spared all from harm, sustained in vigorous health and given the will to do and to hold fast at times when without it the grasp must have slackened and the fight been given up. A word of gratitude to you may yet be added and through you to your right hand, Mr. Pullman, the financial secretary. I was not unmindful of the mental rack upon which you were being daily tried, nor of the heavy responsibility you have carried ; yet you failed not to cheer when the dark days came nor to strengthen and encourage when opportunity

INTERIOR OF GREGORIAN CHURCH AT OORFA.

offered ; so that at times of discouragement which it must be confessed did occur, I could always feel that a double vigil was being kept on my behalf; one in the heart of her who ever asks in my far away home, and one in yours, "Lord, give him wisdom, give fortitude, give patience."

In thus reporting to you, it becomes a pleasure to recall the hospitality so freely offered by many; by Christians and by Moslems, Armenians, Greeks and others who were able to assist. At the different stations of the American Missions our gratitude has been largely drawn upon, for at these we have been treated as brothers. Every one has done all possible for comfort

REV. GEORGE WASHBURN, D. D., PRESIDENT OF ROBERT COLLEGE, BEBEC.

ROBERT COLLEGE.

CISTERN OF THE THOUSAND COLUMNS, STAMBOUL.

WALL TOWER, DIARBEKIR.

and for the furtherance of our work. At Harpoot, where it was my lot to spend many weeks the friendship and moral support received has been and always will be highly valued. At all Consulates on our route, those of our own dear land, those of England and of France, we have been most hospitably welcomed and helped as the occasion gave opportunity. Finally in this connection I recall with most agreeable sensations the reception and warm interest shown in our mission by our countrymen the Admiral and officers of the U. S. Ship San Francisco at Smyrna, and by the officers of the U. S. Ship Marblehead at Mersina.

Respectfully submitted,
E. M. WISTAR.

Constantinople, July 22d, 1896.

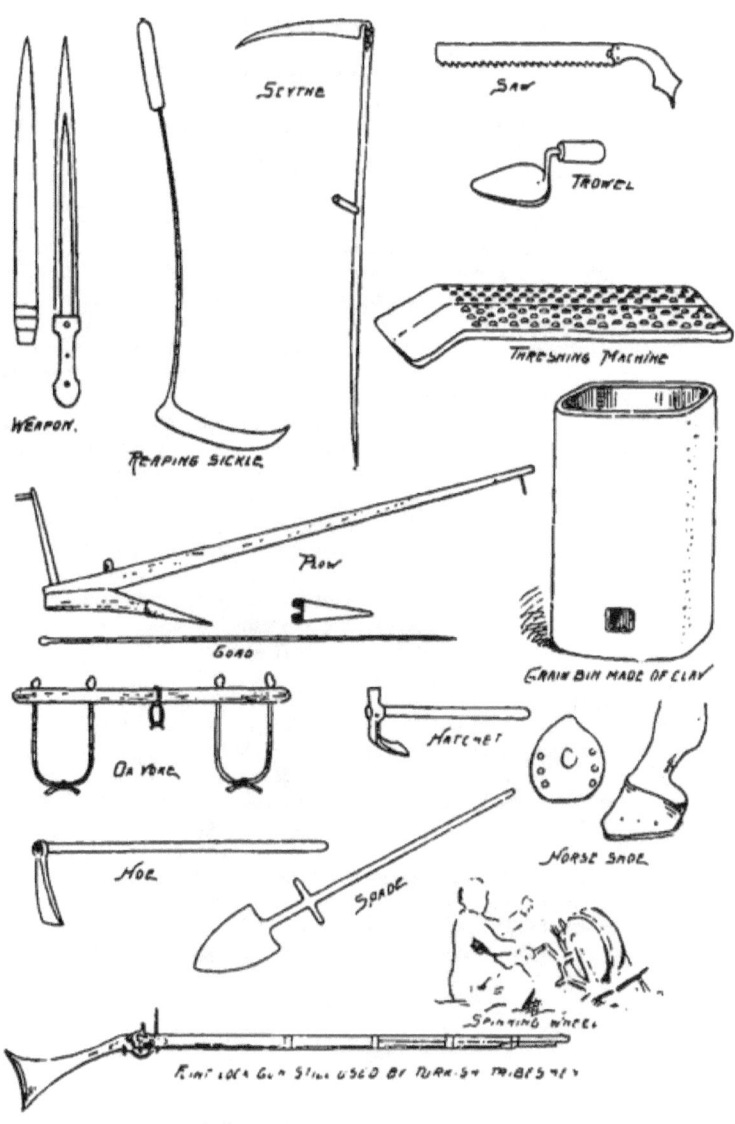

TOOLS, AGRICULTURAL IMPLEMENTS, WEAPONS, ETC.

REPORT OF

CHARLES KING WOOD,

OF PHILADELPHIA, SPECIAL FIELD AGENT, IN CHARGE
OF THIRD EXPEDITION.

To Miss CLARA BARTON, President:

On the 19th of last March your second expedition, under Edward M. Wistar and myself, with dragomen, left Constantinople for Alexandretta with supplies and funds, following closely upon the first expedition under Dr. Hubbell. At that time, although provided with *teskeres* (Turkish passports) the way was not entirely clear for our further progress toward the interior. But on arriving at the port of entry, through the efforts of Daniel Walker, Esq., our American Consular Agent, ably seconded by your own influence at the Capital, we were enabled to have our papers *viséd* for Aintab. Thus, step by step, at first scarcely knowing one day if we should be in a position to advance the next, we made our way toward the stricken districts. The journey was rough and not unaccompanied by hardships and dangers. Now that it is all over we can only remember the joy of having been permitted to be of some little service to our fellow men and to her also whose whole life has been spent in extending the helping hand, and never an empty one, to the afflicted and destitute of no matter what name or creed. In this joy we forget the trials that appear less and less as we regard them in retrospect.

Dr. Hubbell had just dispatched several large caravans with clothing, tools and other supplies to Marash, Aintab, and other points in the field, and without loss of time on the day following our arrival in Alexandretta we set out for Aintab with an escort of Turkish soldiers. I may take this occasion to say that under all circumstances the Ottoman authorities have insured us the most efficient protection. During all the four months spent in the interior we were never without a guard for a moment—they were sometimes embarassingly in evidence. One had little privacy and could not even go for a bath without being accompanied by a zaptieh, but I have no doubt that the safety of our lives and property was due to these precautions. The country is infested with brigands, overrun with nomadic tribes of Kourds, Arabs, and by errant bands of Circassians, so without an armed escort of soldiers it would be impossible for travelers to penetrate into the interior. Their presence was a badge of official recognition and even the most intrepid marauders have a wholesome fear of government authority.

As we moved on to Aintab we saw many terrified refugees, fleeing to the coast in the hope of embarking on some vessel. There was a spirit of fear and unrest in the air almost palpable in its intensity. Our guards kept us close together, scrutinized carefully every approaching caravan and bunch of travellers, and appeared anxious. At Kurrig-Khan, a little village where we halted one day at noon to rest our animals, we found that only the night before a band of Circassians had planned to attack the place and plunder the inhabitants, but the authorities had gotten hold of the intent and forestalled it, by dispatching post-haste a squad of Turkish infantry to protect the village.

Approaching Killis, rumors came to us of troubles in that city, and when we reached there, openly menaced and hooted at by the rabble, we found the ill news was only too true. An uprising had taken place in the city, many people were slain, and shops and houses had been plundered. There was no room for us in the khan, even among the cattle and camels, so we were obliged to seek shelter elsewhere, and as we went through the narrow winding streets every shop was empty and every door barred. The business life was gone from the city and excitement was written on every face. Finally, however, we found another khan, difficult of access and dirty, and entered only by an intricate passage-way, almost a *cul-de-sac*, but it was our only haven and we had to make the best of it. We remained two days in Killis purchasing supplies, &c., and notwithstanding the riot about us, were entirely protected and unharmed.

The governor of the city sent his "salaams" and inquired as to our personality and intentions. To this we responded by a call of courtesy, giving him the desired information and extending our thanks for the protection which had been afforded us during such troubled times. We found that his Excellency had known of our approach several days, that he had received instructions to take care of us and had acted upon them.

Leaving Killis in the early morning, our long caravan strung out single-file over the foot-hills and into the mountains, a brave sight and one that I am sure that could they have seen it would have delighted the hearts of the charitable Americans, whose contributions were thus finding a way to the desolated homes of Anatolia. The "trail" (there was no road) was tortuous and muddy, and for much of the way among huge boulders. Up and down over mountains and valleys uninhabited, and almost uninhabitable, treeless, stony wastes. For miles the only signs of human life were bands of Kourds or wandering Gypsies, and flocks of cattle, sheep and goats, with the wild looking skin-clad shepherds who led them in search of the scanty herbage that grows in the springtime among this chaos of rocks. A wierd, monotonous country, a wilderness and the picture of desolation! One can readily imagine true the tales of robbery or worse, upon these lonely mountain sides. It is marvellous to see how the long legged, awkward camels with their heavy loads manage to tread their way over such rough trails. Silently and slowly they move along like the ghosts of dead creatures, and yet, they are the best means of conveying merchandise in this land of primitive conveniences.

RED CROSS HEADQUARTERS, FARKIN, WOOD'S EXPEDITION.
CASTLE BELONGING TO A KOURDISH BEY.

At Aintab we remained a week gathering information relative to the needs of the people, which as you know we have reported to you from time to time; and arranging for the distribution of our caravan loads. And then leaving Dr. Hubbell's expedition we pressed on several days further east to Beredjik upon the Euphrates, another city which has suffered much but where it did not appear practicable to establish a station.

At Oorfa, our next place of importance, we found Miss Shattuck, assisted by Mr. Saunders, in charge of the relief work. Miss Shattuck was entirely alone in Oorfa during the never-to-be-forgotten days of December 28th and 29th. The brave part she played in saving so many lives is too well known to need reiteration, but I cannot refrain from expressing the sentiments that we cherish toward her, as those of sincere admiration for her Christian character and noble heroism, with an affectionate remembrance of her many sisterly kindnesses, and the hearty hospitality which was so freely extended to us in her home. With the relief work very well systematized, she was looking particularly toward the future, realizing that American and English funds would not always continue to flow in as they were doing. She had a large force of men and women employed daily in an industrial department, making clothing and bedding, which was then distributed among the necessitous; she was also giving weekly rations to extreme cases.

Our work in Oorfa was intended to be supplementary to that already so well established there. We left a fund for the manufacture and distribution of cooking utensils, and for the re-instatement of the various handicrafts of the city such as those in need of tools or small capital. Then we pressed on two days further to Severek, a city smaller than Oorfa but badly in want of aid. Inquiries were made, and as we know, subsequently acted upon. Two long days in the saddle and a part of a third brought us to the ancient walled city of Diarbekir, the Amida which harrassed not a little the ancient Romans. Everywhere from the neighborhood refugees had fled into the city, and the consequence was congestion and direst distress. As we approached we passed several burned and deserted villages where every house had been looted. Although about two thousand people were killed in the city itself and a whole quarter of the bazaars laid waste and everyone plundered, yet the loss was proportionately much less than in the surrounding villages, which had been sacked of absolutely every portable thing they possessed, even to the doors, windows, and timbers of the roofs.

We met the kindest reception from Mr. Cecil M. Hallward, British Consul for the Vilayet of Diarbekir, making his comfortable Consulate our home during the two days we remained in the city. Consul Hallward has been doing what he can to relieve the wants of the people, but with a field of 60,000 needy souls and funds largely inadequate he is handicapped at every turn. Up to that time only 1,575 liras ($8,000) had been received for the entire field from every source. This amount, however, had been augmented at my last visit there (of which more later) to about 5,000 liras ($22,000), still vastly insufficient and proportionately much less than that of any other district. Here, therefore, to the best of my judgment was the greatest need in proportion to the help afforded, that had come under our observation. In the district of Silouan, for instance, where there are twelve thousand indigent, an indigence more desperate than one can possibly imagine, only two hundred liras had been distributed. Over two hundred and twenty persons had died from actual starvation and there was the greatest distress. Forty-eight villages were utterly destroyed, their cattle driven off and all tools and implements stolen. Even should the people return to their ruined houses, they would be impotent to aid themselves without at least the means to purchase materials and implements to recommence their work, and then they must live in the meantime until they can realize on their labors. Thirty-seven hundred shops, one thousand in the city of Diarbekir alone, had been burned or otherwise destroyed. Without ocular evidence, and scarcely then, can one conceive of the fearful destitution in this region. And then there is Nisibin Hiné and Hazere, and in all the devastated district of Mardin and other fields yet untouched, and there was no one to go to them. All this data was secured, and anticipating returning later, we went on to meet Dr. Hubbell according to instructions from yourself. We set out across the rugged, snow-capped Taurus Mountains to the city of Harpoot, where we arrived three days later. Here we again divided our forces and it was my lot to go to Palou, lying two days' over the mountains in a gorge of the Euphrates. Here was a field embracing besides the city of Palou, fifty-eight villages with a population of perhaps fifty thousand souls, of which at least fifteen thousand were destitute. There are more than two hundred villages in the Palou field, a large part of which are Kourd or Turk. The people are barbarous and still in part ruled over by feudal chiefs who hold almost despotic sway over the lives, honor, and property of their vassals. Palou suffered greatly during the massacres, and through fear the local committee appointed by the missionaries was unable to distribute aid to the people. Here was another place where the greatest need prevailed and which only the Red Cross was able to reach. Accordingly, with Professor Tenekegian from the Mission college at Harpoot, a most capable assistant and interpreter, we lost no time in repairing to the scene of action. The pale, emaciated faces and tattered garments of the people bore only abundant testimony that we arrived none too soon. We plunged at once into personal work, preparing first as a foundation for all just and proper distribution, careful lists of families, eliminating all such as were in any way able to care for themselves or had friends in America, Constantinople, or elsewhere to aid them, and cutting down the number in a family considered as needy to the very lowest point, with a view to making the funds we had achieve the greatest possible help to the greatest number. A committee of the best men of the place was appointed to meet with us and go over these lists and revise and correct them before we should give out any supplies, so that when the distributions commenced we were certain that they were fair and equal and that none who were worthy were omitted. Three thousand articles of clothing and bedding were distributed from headquarters in the city. One thousand large pieces of cloth suitable either for clothing or bedding were also distributed. Employment was given to all the blacksmiths, iron being furnished them for which they paid us market price out of the value of the tools which they made. Over three thousand plows, scythes, shovels, saws, pickaxes, and other implements were manufactured and distributed among the fifty-eight villages and the city in accordance with our lists. Assistance was also afforded for the purchase of some six hundred work-cattle, and for the rebuilding of several thousand destroyed houses. One hundred and fifty new widows were supplied with wool or cotton and spinning-wheels also, with which they are enabled to earn their own living and that of the orphans dependent upon them. Scores of other women were employed daily at headquarters cutting out garments and bedding, or spinning thread which we gave with the articles for the people to sew for themselves. Three hundred artisans were re-established in their usual avocations. The water-way to the destroyed quarter of the city had become sadly in need of repair, affording but a feeble, largely insufficient flow, thus threatening severe distress and probably disease during the coming heated term. This we undertook to repair, giving work to needy men and at the same time bestowing a most important boon upon the city. It was commenced at our very entrance into the field, and it was a most happy forerunner, for Moslem and Christian alike in the Orient regard one who gives a supply of water to the people as little lower than the angels. So our initial stroke was a propitious one and we soon found that the prayers of all were rising in our behalf because of it. When the repairs were finished the people said that never since the building of the aqueduct had they obtained so copious a water supply.

The relief work included in its scope absolutely every needy family in the whole field; there was not an individual to whom something was not given, and that something, be it clothing or bedding, plow, saw or shovel, assistance in business or what it might, was to the best of our knowledge the thing the most essential for each one. The authorities were kind and visited us often, but never once did they interfere with our work or seek to control our methods, and the "lists" from which we distributed were not prepared by the Turkish Government but by ourselves. We asked directly upon entering the work that the Governor would appoint a commission of Turkish officials to be present at all distributions as a protection to ourselves; but the commission did not long attend our lengthy sittings, and it ended in our simply sending in to the Governor occasional reports as to what distributions we had made.

In addition to other work we distributed a food supply of 97,056 piastres from missionary relief funds, among the villages and the city of Palou. Five hard toilsome weeks were spent in Palou, but finally when we mounted our horses to ride away, it was a grateful sight to remark the increased activity in the market places and to see that the pinched and suffering look

HARPOOT RUINS.

SECTION OF RED CROSS CARAVAN.

GALATA TOWER, OR THE TOWER OF CHRIST, WAS BUILT IN 1348.
NOW USED AS A FIRE STATION.

had almost faded away from the faces of the people and a renewed hope and resolution had taken its place. With the courage born of the fact that some one from the outside world had come to them and knew and appreciated their condition, they had aroused themselves from the fearful apathy into which they had fallen, and with the opportunities that the Red Cross had afforded them they were now getting on their feet again. We were assured over and over that if the Red Cross had only come to them and done nothing, the moral effect of its presence alone was invaluable. As we rode out over the plains of Palou on our return journey with our labors ended, we saw farmers working in the fields with oxen and plows that we had given them, some with our picks and shovels clearing away the debris from their demolished houses and others rebuilding with Red Cross timbers. One man I remember we met on the road with a great blacksmith's bellows that our money had bought for him, and so it was all along the road. We were gratified by seeing the ripened fruits of our

OLD TOWER AT OORFA.

labors, meeting on every hand the prayers and benedictions from grateful hearts; some even endeavoring to kiss our hands and our feet in the exuberance of their feeling. The harvest was ripe for the sickle and we were glad that our aid and tools had been timely given.

Reaching Harpoot again only one day was spent in preparation, and then with Baron Vartan, a young native teacher as interpreter and assistant (Kourdish was the only language of the new field to which we were going, so a new interpreter had to be secured), we set out for Diarbekir, and the devastated district of Silouan; for the Vilayet of Diarbekir had all the while lived in memory and lain both heavily and hopefully on my heart. Perhaps even yourself will never realize the joy with which I received your brief order—"Take 1,000 liras and go to Diarbekir." We knew that close behind that was the general order to report to Constantinople at a given time. Not a moment of either day or night was lost, as you may well imagine. Starting in the afternoon we traveled all night, the next day and the next night, reaching Diarbekir in little over 48 hours, a journey ordinarily requiring from three to four days. Stopping in the city only one night, we ordered to be made by the smiths 1,400 artisan, farm and other tools, and then hastened on to Farkin, the principal town of Silouan to establish a relief station. Fording the Tigris, for two days we journeyed eastward over a monotonous, rolling country, almost deserted—only here and there the little mud hamlets of Kourds. A village was but a crumbling pile of ruined walls, deserted and a nesting place only for the storks. In perhaps a dozen of these villages we saw not so much as one house with even a roof. But the saddest sight of all to me was the miles and miles of fallow ground. Scarcely a plowed field, except those about the Kourd settlements, in all that vast territory over which we traveled. What famine! What misery! Even worse if possible does this foretell for another year! Once a rich, thriving and populous land, and to what has it come? The cradle of our race, and look at it now. We arrived only in the nick of time with our harvest tools; we found people in the fields *actually endeavoring to garner the grain with their naked hands.* Fancy, if possible, such an utterly destitute condition; it is well nigh incredible and pitiable beyond expression. Fancy if you can the joy of the people at the advent of the Red Cross in their midst.

Upon reaching Farkin, the Centurion or head of our body-guard, took us directly to the Government House to pay our respects to the Governor, and also that we might give some account of ourselves. His Excellency, evidently forewarned of our arrival, received us with great cordiality, and offered us the hospitality of one of the Beys of the Vilayet—a Kourd chief—which suggestion was promptly ratified by Hadji Raschid Agha himself. Shortly we found ourselves quartered in his great stone house, built on the massive inner walls of the ancient Meafarkin. He had many servants, fine picturesque looking fellows with long straight knives in their girdles, and these, his whole household and stables he placed at our disposal, giving us the keys. We all slept on the roof together under the bright rainless Oriental night sky, and we were made as comfortable as courtesy could suggest. A dinner even was given in our honor, and many of the Turkish grandees were in attendance.

As we had only a short time to remain in Farkin, we went to work at once to appoint and instruct a committee, consisting of one Gregorian, one Roman Catholic, one Syrian and one Protestant, to receive and distribute tools when we should be gone. We told them if there was any interference with their work, or if the Kourds plundered any of the implements, that fact was to be immediately reported to consul Hallward at Diarbekir, who kindly assured me that he was prepared to take measures in such an event to compel restitution and to prevent further difficulties in that direction.

We saw half of the implements actually in the hands of the committee and the others on the way, and then returned to Diarbekir and left the balance of the funds, which time did not permit to distribute in person, under the direction of the English Consul for further relief in Farkin and in Redwap, another sadly needy neighboring district.

We then set out again on the long tiresome week's journey over the heated plains and rough mountain trails of Mesopotamia back again to Harpoot, where we found our good friend and co-worker, Edward M. Wistar, having finished a glorious campaign in that field, and in readiness for departure for Constantinople, in response to your call for consultation and rest.

We were glad when our responsibility was over, and it was with light hearts that we started on the long ride of two weeks to the coast at Samsoun, and then two days longer by steamer on the Black Sea, down the Bosphorus to you, and Mr. Pullman, the tireless faithful secretary, the brotherly co-worker, to whose energy and competency we all owe so much. What a pleasure it was to be once more by your side and to clasp your hand in warm greeting mingled with the affection you know and appreciate as well as we can tell you.

And now my little story, as the fairy books would say, is ended, and I beg leave to close my very informal report with sincerest thanks for the privilege which has been accorded me of allying my humble services to the noble ranks of the American National Red Cross.

Constantinople, August 1st, 1896.   CHARLES KING WOOD.

A BIT OF PALOU.

REPORT OF

DR. IRA HARRIS,

OF TRIPOLI, SYRIA, PHYSICIAN IN CHARGE OF THE FOURTH FIELD EXPEDITION FOR THE RELIEF OF MARASH AND ZEITOUN.

Dr. Ira Harris, resident American physician at Tripoli, Syria, a gentleman of high attainments, Christian character, scholarship and service, who directs a large private hospital and practice of his own, honored the Red Cross and contributed largely to the beneficence of his and our own people's efforts to relieve and rebuild the people of Asia Minor, by accepting a commission to command an expedition for the relief of the fever-stricken thousands, residents and refugees, crowded into the cities of Marash and Zeitoun. The reports received from consuls and missionaries presented a terrible condition of affairs, threatening the lives of thousands by pestilence and hunger, more rapidly than the Circassian knife and the Kourdish spear and bullet had done. Our own special agents were all in charge of difficult and distant fields, and none could be spared to this section. After various disappointments, aided by the Rev. Dr. Post at Beyrout Dr. Ira Harris was reached and asked to aid in organizing and forming a relief expedition at once. Besides himself as director, six other physicians and two pharmacists were required. Dr. Harris, though burdened with hospital patients and promised operations, finally decided to proceed to Beyrout and meet Dr. Post, taking with him his own assistant and pharmacist. Dr. Hubbell had already been Dr. Harris' guest and this fact aided the latter's acceptance. At Beyrout time was spent in examining medical applicants, most of whom withdrew however on learning of the dangers before them. Two Protestant doctors were secured on the second day, and so with half the needed medical force at hand, the supplies and stores were quickly purchased and packed for travel. Arrangements at Tripoli for the care of Dr. Harris' own patients were then made, and upon the third of April our fourth expedition was under way. A route was chosen via

Mersene and Adana. At the latter city some delay was occasioned by the rumors of incursions of bandit tribes to neighboring towns and villages and an insufficient military escort available. After trying in vain two or three days, to influence the local authorities Dr. Harris telegraphed to Red Cross headquarters for assistance. The matter was immediately brought to the attention of the Porte, through the U. S. Legation, and within an hour an imperial order was sent to the Governor of Adana. As fine a mounted Turkish soldier guard as ever escorted an expedition was at once found, and Dr. Harris with his corps of assistants, hastened on to Marash, where he was welcomed by Dr. Hubbell of our first expedition, on the eighteenth of April, after five days' of severe travel. Dr. Harris' report was embodied in a letter. After enumerating the trials at Adana, from which he was so quickly freed by the order from the Porte, the doctor continues:

We found that the medical work was being cared for by native physicians, and the missionaries and their wives were caring for the other relief work, one feature of which seemed to me very valuable indeed, *i. e.*, the making of clothing by poor women from the material sent by you from Constantinople or purchased by Dr. Hubbell in Marash. I wish the dear people in America who gave of their means, could see with their own eyes the condition of thousands in these districts alone. The hundreds of women, almost destitute of covering, and that a mass of rags. It does not require much thought to realize the value of good clothing at such a time.

A consultation was held and our party decided to proceed to Zeitoun, just as soon as our weary bodies were rested. Unfortunately the day after we arrived I had a severe chill and fever which prostrated me for several days. As the symptoms seemed to resemble typhus fever the doctors remained with me until a clear diagnosis was made by the fever leaving me on Thursday. The next day the party went to Zeitoun with Mr. Macallum, I following three days later.

I have witnessed scenes of suffering, both in the United States and the Orient, but never, to my dying day, will I be able to dismiss from my mind the horror of the pinched, haggard faces and forms that gathered about me that first day. Before we left the tent one of the doctors said: "we will now see the place is full of walking skeletons." This expressed fully their condition. Just imagine a place having a normal population of 12,500 living all told in 1,403 houses, you can see there is not much cubic space to spare; then imagine 7,000 or more refugees to be provided for in the town also. Some of the Zeitounes gave shelter to a small number, but the greater majority lived on the street, under the houses, in many instances too vile to be of use to its owner; in cow and donkey stables with the animals; in spaces in close proximity to water closets; in fact not a place that even suggested shelter was unoccupied. The smell and presence of human excrement were everywhere, and this, added to divers other odors made the air a fit place for the culture of disease germs. So much for the hygienic conditions of the place.

DISEASES. I regret that I am unable to give the exact number of those afflicted with each individual disease; to ascertain this would have taken too much valuable time. We found it a difficult task even to make a true estimate of the number ill with acute diseases. Our first estimate sent you, viz: 1,400 dysentery and diarrhœa, 600 typhus fever, afterwards proved nearly correct, *i. e.*, if we take about 300 from the typhus and add to the dysentery. These were acute cases. Of the refugees, ninety-eight per cent. complained and were treated for diseases such as chronic dysentery, diarrhœa, dropsy (usually those recovering from typhus), rheumatism, bronchitis, dyspepsia, malaria; all were suffering from anæmia and debility.

CAUSES. Overcrowding and bad air; but that condition bordering on starvation was the principal cause of all the sickness. I should add, many of the cases of diarrhœa were caused from eating a soup made from grass, weeds, buds and leaves of shrubs and trees. In fact anything green that could be gathered in the fields was boiled in water to which a small quantity of flour was added. This diet was especially dangerous to children.

TREATMENT. We were soon convinced that if we expected to gain the upper hand of all this sickness and save even a remnant of the refugees, we must first feed the sick, and then when they were well—to give the former every possible chance to get well, and to prevent the well from becoming ill. Second, we must try in every way in our power to get the refugees to return to their homes, or at all events to camp out in the fields. The first day we filled the hospital opened by consul Barnum with cases off the street, and from that time on we increased hospital facilities as fast as possible. We engaged two men and one woman to care for the hospital; four interpreters and one assistant for the pharmacist. We then divided the town into districts so as to systematically get at every sick person. Then we hired (for we could get nothing without a system of bargaining as to price) two large copper kettles used to make grape molasses, and purchased two hundred pounds of beef and made a strong, rich soup. We then strained every nerve to get a soup ticket into the possession of every sick person. We did not waste time by trying to cull out the impostors; in fact there were very few of this class, *all* the refugees were needy and hungry. The second day we added three kettles, and to supply the number we served at 10 o'clock clear meat broth; at 4 o'clock thick soup of beef and rice. By the end of the third day every sick person was receiving food. Then all complaints of vomiting the medicine ceased.

The problem then to be met was—how to get the people to go outside the town. We suggested that if they would, we would place a soup kettle out in the open fields to the south, north and east, and in addition to the soup we would give them flour. This had a very decided effect, for 1,000 went the first day. The moving continued until every person living on the streets and in cow stables had built for themselves shelters of twigs and leaves. Now the butchers saw a chance of applying the plan of putting up the price of meat from seven to fourteen piasters per oke (2¾ lbs.). But we had anticipated this and sent men to a friendly Moslem village to purchase cattle. So their scheme failed. By the end of the second week there were no hungry people in Zeitoun.

RESULTS. The typhus cases began to recover, the new cases took on a mild form, the same could be said of dysentery. The new cases of both became less and less until they almost disappeared. The most marked improvement was the rapidity which the daily funerals in the three burying grounds decreased. I watched these places with deep interest, for they were a thermometer to gauge the success of our work, and it was with deep gratitude to God that we saw the daily burials reduced from fifteen to none. So much for the acute cases. The first week the chronic cases took the entire time of one doctor, each taking our regular turn. Tonic treatment and food so reduced the number that sixty became the daily average at the end of the second week. At the end of the third week, fell to ten. Our pharmacist, Shickri Fakhuri, proved as he always has, a jewel. His hands were full to prepare the prescriptions of three doctors. At first it was necessary for one of us to give him assistance of an hour or so daily. On the 20th of May, we felt we could leave the town free of acute typhus and dysentery. We gave to the committee selected by Mr. Macallum, funds enough to keep the soup kettles going for one week, and 200 liras ($880) worth of flour, which would suffice for at least six weeks, and by that time it was hoped that all the refugees would have departed for their homes.

On our return to Marash we remained four days superintending the work of relief of the native doctors, and performing surgical operations. We then started for the coast. We chose a shorter and less expensive route than that by which we came. We were able in several places on the road to give needed relief, although to a limited amount. The lessons learned by our experience have been many:

1st. The value of keeping well, for obviously, success depends upon this. It is evident to us the way to reduce the danger of infection to a minimum for medical men, is to eat and sleep outside the infected town. This plan may present difficulties, but if possible, it is best. The dreadful mortality among doctors and nurses in the epidemics of typhus fever is well known. The query is, could not this mortality be reduced by the plan suggested? It proved so in our case at least.

2d. The food supply is of first importance, especially for epidemics caused by *lack* of food.

3d. The utter worthlessness of medication without it.

4th. Pure air. It is much better for people to risk possible exposure out in the open air, than risk contagion in vile unwholesome shelter in an overcrowded town.

Lastly, I am more than ever convinced that small doses of medicine oft repeated give better results in typhus and dysentery than those usually recommended in text books. I, at least, had ample opportunity to test this to my satisfaction.

In conclusion, I wish to express my hearty approval of the methods pursued by yourself and associates, especially as applied to the giving relief to the suffering people. The distribution of your forces was admirable, and the way they grasped the situation and the needs of the people of each particular place should excite the admiration of all who have the relief of this afflicted people at heart. Instead of scattering the money here and there in an aimless way, food, medical and surgical supplies, clothing, seed, cattle, farming utensils, simple cooking vessels, were systematically distributed, thus putting all in the way of providing for themselves in the future and becoming independent again. It is very easy to pauperize the people of the Orient, but your methods prevent this.

Again, the non-sectarian aspect of your work has made a favorable impression. It eliminates all religious prejudices from the minds of all, especially the religious heads. Therefore no ungenerous remarks as to the ulterior motives of your relief. On the contrary we heard nothing but words of commendation.

No one but yourself and your associates and those who have lived in Turkey for a number of years, can appreciate the difficulties and perplexities under which you have labored from the very first.

I am sorry that this report ends my official relations with you, but believe me, dear Miss Barton, my wife and I shall hold yourself and your associates always in interested remembrance.

Truly and sincerely yours,

IRA HARRIS.

Tula, Mt. Lebanon, August 15, 1896.

ARMENIAN VILLAGE OF OULASCH, NEAR SIVAS.

MARASH.

EGIN, THE HILLSIDE COVERED WITH MULBERRY TREES.

KOURDISH MOUNTAIN VILLAGE.

RELIEF FIELD TELEGRAMS AND REPLIES,

WITH OTHER MATTER.

[ORIGINAL.]

[Ottoman Turkish handwritten text]

[TRANSLATION.]

Arabkir May 17 1896

Miss Barton,

Since three days we are attending with our doctors and their attendants to one hundred sick per day. The contagious fever Typhus is diminishing. Miss Bush and all the party are distributing clothing and bedding. Seneca is giving implements and seed to the farmers. The needs here are extreme. Wistar's party are at Egin Wood with his party are working in the district of Palou.

Hubbell

HEADING USED ON ALL TURKISH TELEGRAMS.

TELEGRAMS.

To afford a comprehensive idea of the methods employed in carrying on our work in Asia Minor, we give a transcript of the the telegrams sent and received while our expeditions were in the field.

As all or nearly all messages were in Turkish or Arabic, the translations were, at times, very dissimilar to the original telegrams.

We give a fac-simile on the opposite page of an ordinary message, with the translation. As interpreters were sometimes difficult to find, one can readily imagine a small disadvantage in working among strange people with a strange language.

Of the hundred or thereabouts of cablegrams connected with the work, received from and sent to America, no mention is made at the present time.

TELEGRAMS.

Constantinople, March 8, 1896.

BARTON (S. E.), New York.

Shipped large quantities supplies *via* Alexandretta, caravan, interior, yesterday. Sent funds to Harpoot, Sivas, Marash. Pressing needs increasing, wire all parties. BARTON.

(This cablegram is given to show the starting of the expeditions. Between this and the next dispatch of the 20th, from Dr. Hubbell at Alexandretta, two shipments were made and the second expedition formed and left.)

Alexandretta, March 20, 1896.

BARTON, care American Legation, Constantinople.

Arrived safely. We and goods expect to go forward.

HUBBELL.

Constantinople, March 20, 1896.

HUBBELL, Alexandretta, Syria.

Greetings. Wistar's party sailed yesterday. All well except Mrs Mason. Telegraph your needs. BARTON.

Marash, March 20, 1896.

Miss BARTON, Constantinople.

As at Marash and Zeitoun fatal diseases of dysentery and —————— are raging, we are requesting from Beyrout six physicians and two apothecaries, with medicines and necessary appurtenances. Can you defray the expenses? LEE, MACALLUM, SHEPARD.

(Received March 23. This dispatch being in Turkish the names of the other diseases given could not be made out.)

Constantinople, March 24, 1896.

LEE, Marash.

I will gladly defray expenses if within our means. Approximate smallest amount required. BARTON.

Constantinople, March 25, 1896.

Dr. J. B. HUBBELL, Alexandretta, Syria, care Daniel Walker (consular agt.)

Mrs. Mason died peacefully at three this morning. We will carry out Ernest's wishes if possible. Wire suggestions or advice. Have cabled Satolli. BARTON.

Alexandretta, March 28, 1896.

CLARA BARTON, American Legation, Constantinople.

Wistar's party here. We all start Aintab to-morrow in company with Doctor Fuller. The goods were sent Monday.

HUBBELL.

Marash, March 30, 1896.

CLARA BARTON, Constantinople.
　Physicians for four hundred liras, Turkish, necessary.
　　　　　　　　　　　　　　　　　　　　　　　　　LEE.

Beyrout, March 30, 1896.

BARTON, Constantinople.
　Ready. Cannot send expedition until I receive credit two hundred pounds.
　　　　　　　　　　　　　　　　　　　　　　　　　POST.

Constantinople, March 30, 1896.

DR. GEORGE E. POST, Beyrout.
　Have just telegraphed you two hundred liras Ottoman bank. Wire when physicians leave. Please write particulars.
　　　　　　　　　　　　　　　　　　　　　　　　　BARTON.

Constantinople, March 30, 1896.

LEE, American, Marash.
　Your telegram received. Will pay four hundred liras if necessary. Have cabled Dr. Post two hundred liras. Courage. Physicians start Marash immediately.
　　　　　　　　　　　　　　　　　　　　　　　　　BARTON.

Constantinople, March 30, 1896.

HUBBELL, care Dr. Fuller, Aintab.
　Six physicians, two apothecaries with supplies leave Beyrout for Marash, probably to-day, our expense. Typhus, small-pox, dysentery, epidemic there. Yourself and men forbidden to enter into contagion. You are needed outside to supply those who must be there. Answer quick.
　　　　　　　　　　　　　　　　　　　　　　　　　BARTON.

Constantinople, March 31, 1896.

HUBBELL, American, Aintab.
　Send two-thirds caravan to Lee, Marash, at once. Confer with Shepard concerning Marash, if at Aintab. Push on to Harpoot. Orders issued furnishing every facility for distribution. Success depends on prompt action. We ship more goods next steamer.
　　　　　　　　　　　　　　　　　　　　　　　　　BARTON.

Constantinople, April 3, 1896.

DR. FULLER, Aintab.
　Where are our men? Why don't they report? Answer paid.
　　　　　　　　　　　　　　　　　　　　　　　　　BARTON.

TELEGRAMS.

Constantinople, April 3, 1896.

DANIEL WALKER, Alexandretta.
Where are our men? Did they leave with Fuller? When? Answer.

BARTON.

(Just in this interval, between Alexandretta and Aintab, had occurred the massacre at Killis, which news, together with the inquiries of the government for the routes taken was giving us great anxiety.)

Constantinople, April 3, 1886.

DR. POST, Beyrout.
Cabled you two hundred liras, thirtieth, no word. Where are physicians? Wait for nothing, wrote you yesterday. BARTON.

Constantinople, April 3, 1896.

DR. SHEPARD, Aintab.
Have ordered and paid for eight physicians to Marash. Have they reported? Where are our men? If at Aintab please send some of them to Marash with supplies at once. Answer paid. BARTON.

Constantinople, April 4, 1896.

LEE, American, Marash.
What goods and in what quantity do you most need? We will send them if possible. BARTON.

(This telegram was answered by letter and goods sent.)

Aintab, April 4, 1896.

BARTON, Constantinople.
We arrived on Wednesday. The authorities gave us a splendid reception. We have received your telegram. We are sending goods to Marash. We will be on the twenty-fifth at Harpoot; and by way of Oorfa, Diarbekir, Marash. We will start for Malatia. HUBBELL.

(It was sometimes impossible to get a really sensible translation. The above is a specimen.)

Alexandretta, April 6, 1896.

MISS BARTON, through Am. Bible House.
Your men left with Fuller on twenty-eighth. WALKER.

Beyrout, April 6, 1896.

BARTON, through Am. Embassy.
Doctors sailed Friday. POST.

Constantinople, April 8, 1896.

LEE, American, Marash.
    Doctors left Friday. What is present condition epidemics?
BARTON.

Constantinople, April 8, 1896.

HUBBELL, care Dr· Fuller, Aintab.
    Telegram received. Good. So glad. Will ship more goods next steamer. Doctors gone to Marash. Telegraph me every opportunity, both caravans; keep us informed of all, we need it. Let us know your wants. (Will Dr. Fuller please forward?)
BARTON.

Constantinople, April 9, 1896.

DR. POST, Beyrout.
    We cabled money thirtieth; will mail the other two hundred when you desire. Glad doctors have sailed. Please wire arrival. Many thanks.
CLARA BARTON.

Marash, April 10, 1896.

BARTON, Constantinople.
    The sickness is continuing to increase.
LEE.

Beyrout, April 10, 1896.

BARTON.
    Two more doctors willing, shall I send them?
POST.

Constantinople, April 11, 1896.

POST, Beyrout.
    Send physicians by all means. Will send Ltq. 220 by post to-day,
BARTON.

Oorfa, April 11, 1896.

    Arrived at Oorfa all right. How much money can you send?
WISTAR.

Adana, April 11, 1896.

CLARA BARTON, Constantinople.
    Our party of physicians from Beyrout detained here, unable to obtain escort.
HARRIS.

Constantinople, April, 11, 1896.

DR. IRA HARRIS, Adana.
    Turkish Foreign Minister just ordered escort for you. Please let me know if you do not go on at once.
CLARA BARTON.

TELEGRAMS.

Constantinople, April 11, 1896.

Lee, American, Marash.

Thanks for dispatch. Two more physicians ordered from Beyrout. Telegraph conditions often and fully. Will refund all expenses.

BARTON.

(To insure greater security in transmission of messages the word "American" was placed after the name of person addressed.)

Constantinople, April 11, 1896.

Wistar, American, Oorfa.

Telegram received. Very glad. Wire fully all conditions. Send two hundred liras Oorfa next week. Answer; fifteen words paid.

BARTON.

Marash, April 12, 1896.

Barton, Constantinople.

When may we expect doctors here and in the villages? Help is needed in Zeitoun. Three thousand sick and only one doctor. The English consul is ill with typhus. We may hire a doctor from here. All well.

HUBBELL.

(Dr. Hubbell's notes leaving Aintab on the fifth say: "Three days through rain and snow brought us to Marash," where he waited the arrival of Dr. Harris.)

Beyrout, April 12, 1896.

Barton, Constantinople.

Please telegraph second two hundred pounds; have already distributed seventy. Remainder sum nearly due.

POST.

Constantinople, April 14, 1896.

Dr. Post, Beyrout.

Freyer, American Press, will hand you two hundred sterling. Hope the doctors will leave at once. Great need in Zeitoun.

BARTON.

Constantinople, April 13, 1896.

Wistar, American, Oorfa.

Takes twenty-four days to send money Oorfa. Shall we send you there or Harpoot. Answer quick.

BARTON.

DISTRIBUTING SPINNING WHEELS AT ARABKIR.

AINTAB.

CONSTANTINOPLE DOGS.

SECTION OF THE OUTER WALL.

Constantinople, April 14, 1896.

HUBBELL, American, Marash.

Dispatch received. Have sent you money to Harpoot. It will take twenty days to send money to Marash. Shall we send it? Doctors are due there now with medicines. Your party must not remain in contagion. Leave soon as doctors arrive; be careful. All well. BARTON.

Marash, April 14, 1896.

BARTON, Constantinople.

The shops are open here, and money can be used in the purchase of farming implements and other goods. Sickness at Zeitoun increasing; forty or fifty dying there every day. It would be well if you can send medicines quickly. The general conditions in Marash about the same. I want money for Harpoot. HUBBELL.

Constantinople, April 15, 1896.

POST, Beyrout.

Can you purchase large medical supplies and send Marash with doctors? News just reaches us from our own men of terrible condition of epidemic-stricken people. Please send all doctors possible. Draw on us for money required. BARTON.

Constantinople, April 15, 1896.

Dr. WASHBURN, Beyrout.

Please strengthen Dr. Post's efforts in sending doctors and medical supplies to Marash and Zeitoun. We gladly bear all expense. Our men are there.

(Dr. Washburn, president of Robert College, was in Beyrout at this time on business.)

Oorfa, April 15, 1896.

BARTON, Constantinople.

Though delayed, we are received with love everywhere. Distributions at Aintab and Oorfa are going on. Money is sufficient. We shall go to Diarbekir. WISTAR.

Oorfa, April 16, 1896.

BARTON, Constantinople.

Having no vizé from Aintab, we are delayed here. We are looking since four days for the Consul's reply. What are your orders?

WISTAR.

(Owing to neglect on the part of the dragoman the passports were not regular.)

Marash, April 16, 1896.

BARTON, Constantinople.

Harris left Adana. The letters have arrived. Goods are coming. Succeeded in hiring doctor for Marash. Have written.   HUBBELL.

Constantinople, April 17, 1896.

HUBBELL, American, Marash.

One thousand liras for you enroute Harpoot. Five hundred to Macallum, Marash, for you or for the relief committee if you have gone. Borrow from Macallum, if necessary, for your journey. Would advise Harpoot before Malatia unless you have money and supplies with you. Leave Marash soon as doctors arrive. Be careful, keep well. All right here, but very busy. Shall we still ship supplies, if so, what?   BARTON.

Constantinople, April 17, 1896.

WISTAR, American, Oorfa.

Sent two hundred liras to Shattuck for you yesterday, but don't wait for it; Shattuck can use it. Sent five hundred liras to-day for you to Barnum, Harpoot. Very thankful you are doing such splendid work. Keep strong and be careful; all well here. Your letters forwarded to Harpoot.   BARTON.

Oorfa, April 19, 1896.

BARTON, Constantinople.

The instructions in your yesterday's telegram accepted. Your telegram of previous date remains non-translatable.   WISTAR.

(Some telegrams sent and received required days to decipher.)

Marash, April 19, 1896.

BARTON, Constantinople.

Your telegram received, also the five hundred liras. Would suggest as much more for tools. Harris' party arrived yesterday. We start this morning for Malatia. Typhus is increasing here. We are well.   HUBBELL.

Oorfa, April 20, 1896.

BARTON, Constantinople.

Our teskeres have been vizéd. We will be in Harpoot by the thirtieth of April.   WISTAR.

TELEGRAMS.

Constantinople, April 21, 1896.

Dr. Geo. Post, Beyrout.

Letter received; many thanks. Agree with you "no better work than ours possible for suffering humanity irrespective of religious preferences." Cabled you credit two hundred liras to-day. Can you care for medical supplies? Can you find more physicians? Have the two started? Shall we send money to Harris? Can we purchase drugs better here? If so, what kinds? BARTON.

Constantinople, April 21, 1896.

Dr. Harris, Marash.

Rejoiced to learn your arrival. Know you and your corps will attend every detail, refusing assistance to none, whatever his religion or race. How can we best assist your noble work? Please send very frequent reports—daily, if practicable. How many sick? What diseases? What proportion are women? About Zeitoun: Can you attend that city? Where can we obtain more doctors for you? Besides telegraphing reports please write fully your findings at beginning of your work. Classify diseases and and people. Tell us your needs. BARTON.

Marash, April 22, 1896.

Barton, Constantinople.

Been having sharp attack malarial fever. All doctors have left for Zeitoun. Many sick. Will try and go with party to-morrow. Impossible to get more doctors. I post letter to-day. HARRIS.

Beyrout, April 24, 1896.

Barton, Constantinople.

Cable received but no money. In need of funds. Will forward supplies. Am doing all I can. POST.

(Money was sent on 21st but bank did not notify him as usual.)

Constantinople, April 24, 1896.

Post, Beyrout.

Apply Ottoman bank for remittance sent twenty-first, two hundred sterling. PULLMAN.

Marash, April 24, 1896.

Barton, Constantinople.

Party start for Zeitoun to-day.

HARRIS.

Diarbekir, April 25, 1896.

BARTON, Constantinople.
  All well. Vali cordial. Harpoot Wednesday.

WISTAR.

Malatia, April 27, 1896.

BARTON, Constantinople.
  Will leave for Harpoot to-morrow. All well. HUBBELL.

Constantinople, April 28, 1896.

DR. HARRIS, Marash.
  Can send three or four Greek doctors from here, well recommended. Shall we send them? Many thanks for dispatch. How is Zeitoun? America intensely interested in your work. How can we further serve you?

BARTON.

Oorfa, April 29, 1896

BARTON, Constantinople.
  Remittance by pony post is just received. Many thanks.

SHATTUCK.

Aintab, April 29, 1896.

BARTON, Constantinople.
  Typhus and dysentery are raging at Arabkir. The people are in great poverty and the deaths are numerous. Can you send doctors and medicines? SHEPARD.

Constantinople, May 1, 1896.

SHEPARD, American, Aintab.
  We are trying to secure doctors and medicines for Arabkir.

BARTON.

Zeitoun, May 1, 1896.

BARTON, Constantinople.
  We are in need of more doctors. HARRIS.

Constantinople, May 1, 1896.

HUBBELL, American, Harpoot.
  Typhus and dysentery raging at Arabkir. Can you send doctors with medicines from Harpoot? Can you investigate condition of people there without exposing yourself to contagion? Wherever seed is required ask for it of the Turkish Governor; if he cannot furnish it let me know. If you

find places where the people are afraid to go to their fields to cultivate them, report such places to me and measures will be taken here accordingly.
BARTON.

(The above instructions had been just received by me from the Sublime Porte and in all subsequent work were carried out in full.)

Marash, May 3, 1896.

BARTON, Constantinople.

Five hundred pounds received by pony post; we are grateful.
MACALLUM.

(The first five hundred pounds sent Harpoot by pony post was acknowledged by Rev. Dr. Barnum by letter.)

Harpoot, May 4, 1896.

BARTON, Constantinople.

All arrived here Wednesday. Harpoot district including three hundred towns and villages in need of much help. Strong desire for us to remain some weeks here in special work of tools, animals, seeds, shelter and medical relief. Friends here assisting. Advise please. All well.
HUBBELL.

Constantinople, May 5, 1896.

HUBBELL, American, Harpoot.

Telegram received. Very glad. Remain in Harpoot as long as necessary. Wired you Harpoot, May first, concerning sickness in Arabkir; find and answer please. Do you or Wistar need more money now? Report frequently; daily if possible. Much gratified at your line of work. Have cabled your telegram to America.
BARTON.

Zeitoun, May 6, 1896.

BARTON, Constantinople.

We reached here yesterday. The number of refugees is seven thousand, more than half of them are women. Fourteen hundred suffering with —— and dysentery; six hundred have typhus. There are many strangers. I need one hundred liras (?) at once. The hospital work will increase. We will remain here for the present.
HARRIS.

(This telegram was in Arabic and required two days to get even a passable translation.)

Constantinople, May 8, 1896.

HARRIS, American, Zeitoun.

Telegram received. Please do not send in Arabic characters; great difficulty in translating. Have arranged with Peet for Macallum to draw two hundred liras for you at once. Five doctors start for Marash next Monday.

Will report to you for duty. Shall we send medical supplies with them? if so wire kind and quantity. Beautiful letter just received from your wife. Will the five doctors we send be enough for you? We are grateful to you for your heroic efforts.
BARTON.

Harpoot, May 7, 1896.

BARTON, Constantinople.

Wood with assistants goes to Palou district. Wistar with Michael to Tcharsandjak district. A doctor with medicines, Miss Bush, dragoman, Mason, and I to Arabkir. Will need more funds. Wire amount we can have. We buy seed, work cattle, tools, timber for shelter. Conditions for working in fields improving.
HUBBELL.

(The instructions had taken effect.)

Constantinople, May 7, 1896.

HUBBELL, American, Harpoot.

Telegram received. Splendid! Excellent arrangement. So thankful to you all. Have arranged with Peet. Draw fifteen hundred liras from Barnum. We sent one thousand liras in two groups, gold, to Barnum for you and Wistar April 20. Have you received it? if so, acknowledge by wire; anxious. We send five doctors to Harris. Your letters received.
BARTON.

(It became possible for us to transact our money business with the interior by draft at this time. The drafts were sold to merchants. No banks in the interior, all were destroyed.)

Zeitoun, May 12, 1896.

BARTON, Constantinople.

We are very thankful for the money you sent. By our giving food to the famishing sick the sickness is diminishing.
HARRIS.

Harpoot, May 13, 1896.

BARTON, Constantinople.

Three expeditions started as planned. Hubbell's party left for Arabkir to-day. Fifteen hundred liras received by pony post to-day. All well.
GATES.

Palou, May 13, 1896.

BARTON, Constantinople.

We have arrived here and been well received by the Kami-kam.
WOOD.

Tcharsandjak, May 15, 1896.

BARTON, Constantinople.

We had a good reception from the authorities. It is difficult for the industrial instruments (?). They have to be examined from Harpoot. There are plenty of provisions. The country is pretty vast.

WISTAR.

(On receipt of this dispatch the amusing fact occurred to us, viz.: that our great quantities of farming implements in transport to the villages being of iron, were mistaken by the village authorities for arms, which we might be furnishing to the Armenians, and hence delay, and great caution were required. This idea was exploded by the government and the officials instructed that they might trust whatever we furnished. There were no obstructions after this.)

Constantinople, May 16, 1896.

HARRIS, American, Zeitoun.

Four doctors have sailed. They have medicines, nourishing food, disinfecting machines. Ordered to go wherever needed. Much sickness reported north of you.

BARTON.

Tcharsandjak, May 17, 1896.

BARTON, Constantinople.

We are distributing two thousand suits clothing, eight hundred bushels seed, also tools and oxen.

WISTAR.

Palou, May 18, 1896.

BARTON, Constantinople.

In forty villages they need one thousand oxen, which will cost twenty-five hundred liras.

WOOD.

Arabkir, May 18, 1896.

BARTON, Constantinople.

Since three days we are attending with our doctors and their attendants to one hundred sick per day. The contagious fever, typhus, is diminishing. Miss Bush and all the party are distributing clothing and bedding. Our dragoman is giving implements and seed to the farmers. The needs here are extreme. Wistar's party is in Peri. Wood with his men is working in the district of Palou.

HUBBELL.

Constantinople, May 20, 1896.

WOOD, American, Palou.

Investigate and get all information necessary. Do not purchase in large quantities until you hear further from me. Thanks for such splendid work. Take receipts for all purchases.

BARTON.

TELEGRAMS.

Constantinople, May 20, 1896.

HARRIS, Zeitoun.

Your letter just received. Have Macallum draw two hundred liras for the sick. Please "keep the pot boiling." BARTON.

Constantinople, May 20, 1896.

WALKER, Alexandretta.

Cabled you credit Aleppo £50 (liras) to-day. Please give amount to our physicians who will arrive in a few days. BARTON.

Palou, May 21, 1896.

BARTON, Constantinople.

Ten women, eleven men, working daily at headquarters. Nine hundred pieces clothing, two hundred mattress covers. Much silk is being woven. The implements of the villagers are made by blacksmiths. Our work is progressing rapidly. The need of oxen for the villagers is announced from every part. WOOD.

Harpoot, May 24, 1896.

BARTON, Constantinople.

Arrived to-day. Hubbell telegraphed you from Arabkir. 16th, relief proceeding satisfactorily. 17th, wired, obstructions; no reply. Kaimi-kam (governor) at Arabkir, prohibits all intercourse with sick, so we can do nothing for them. He declares no help needed in Arabkir or vicinity.

MASON.

(This matter was at once taken to the Porte, and an order from the Porte sent same day to the governor at Arabkir, which had desired effect instantly.)

Constantinople, May 24, 1896.

HUBBELL, American, Harpoot.

Wood wants cattle; can you instruct him regarding purchase? We can afford two yoke of oxen for each village where necessary. All cattle and tools should be branded or stamped to be owned by us. So glad of your excellent work. Mason's wire here. Porte has ordered all obstructions removed at Arabkir. Will take up Palou with Porte to-morrow.

BARTON.

Constantinople, May 24, 1896.

WOOD, American, Palou.

Can you confer with Hubbell? We can afford two yoke oxen each village, where necessary. Each animal should be branded B. or C. B. All tools stamped with steel die. We must own these things to save them. Take

A COFFEE HOUSE IN PERA.

GROUP OF HAMMALS, SHOWING MANNER OF CARRYING
HEAVY MERCHANDISE.

SECTION OF TURKISH CEMETERY AT SCUTARI.

A HAMMAL.

PLANE TREE OF THE JANIZARIES, STAMBOUL.

TELEGRAMS.

full receipts. Can your blacksmiths make steel dies and branding irons? So glad of your excellent work.   BARTON.

(As we could not brand or stamp with a cross, or U. S., it was decided to use B. or C B., to enable us to trace the relief property in case of robbery or theft.)

Constantinople, May 24, 1896.

WISTAR, Tcharsandjak.

Thanks for excellent letter. Splendid work. Let us know your needs. Can afford two yoke oxen each village where necessary. All cattle should be branded B. or C. B.; all tools stamped same. Can your blacksmiths make steel dies and branding irons?   BARTON,

---

Marash, May 25, 1896.

BARTON, Constantinople.

Start Monday for Alexandretta. Am advising with local doctors here. Feeding the sick and poor soon end the typhus and dysentery. Contagion stamped out.   HARRIS.

Constantinople, May 26, 1896.

HUBBELL, American, Arabkir.

Wired you Harpoot yesterday. Porte has ordered every facility given your work. Wire of any hindrance you meet anywhere. Thankful for your splendid work and your continued health.   BARTON.

Constantinople, May 27, 1896.

WOOD, Palou.

Can you distribute eighty yoke oxen to advantage? Can you purchase them there? At what cost?   BARTON.

Harpoot, May 29, 1896.

BARTON, Constantinople.

Greatest need of oxen; farmers cannot recover without them. Ground must be plowed for fall sowing within twenty days before it dries. Two yoke barely sufficient for two farms. Wood's request moderate.   GATES.

Tcharsandjak, June 1, 1896.

BARTON, Constantinople.

Leave to-day for Harpoot via Palou.   WISTAR.

TELEGRAMS.

Arabkir, May 30, 1896.

BARTON, Constantinople.

Our doctors have attended one thousand sick; one death. We will leave Dr. Hintlian here and we will go next week to Egin and Aghin villages. The local authorities help us on every occasion. We are well.

HUBBELL.

Alexandretta, June 1, 1896.

BARTON, Constantinople.

Off for Tripoli. Doctors returning. Seventy-five pounds handed to Padre for Aintab artisans as you requested. Thanks for good news.

HARRIS.

Constantinople, June 2, 1896.

HUBBELL, American, Arabkir.

Very glad authorities assisting so well. Just wired Gates five thousand liras for all expeditions. Gates wires that cattle must be bought at once to be of use. Think Wistar is with Wood at Palou to-day. He will leave field soon. Met Wheeler and Ellis to-day. Splendid report of your work.

BARTON.

(Dr. Wheeler will be everywhere recognized as the founder and first president of Harpoot College. He lived to see eight of the twelve college buildings go up in flames, and broken with paralysis, a helpless, suffering invalid, he had reached Constantinople on his way back to his own country to die. His death took place in August at his home in Auburndale, Mass.)

> "For the stores of knowledge brought us,
> For the charm thy goodness gave,
> For the lessons thou hast taught us,
> Can we give thee but a grave?"

Constantinople, June 3, 1896.

GATES, American, Harpoot.

Deposited five thousand liras with Peet for you to draw for my men. This makes over forty-three thousand dollars sent Harpoot. Only small balance left for rest of field. Very grateful for all your kindness.

BARTON.

Constantinople, June 2, 1896.

WOOD, American, Palou.

Just wired Gates credit Ltq. 5,000 for all the expenditures. This makes over $43,000 sent Harpoot. You must all use to the best advantage. Use some in Diarbekir province if possible. Brand your cattle and stamp your tools. Wistar wires that he goes to Harpoot *via* Palou; confer together and wire me your plans distinctly. If Wistar must go to London, cannot you remain? Hard to spare you both just now. Hubbell goes to Egin this week.

BARTON.

TELEGRAMS.

Constantinople, June 2, 1896.

FONTANA, British Consul, Harpoot.

Several days ago Porte, at my request, ordered local authorities at Arabkir and Palou to instantly remove all obstructions to the work. Are my men now meeting difficulties anywhere? If so, I will again notify the Porte. May I ask you to consult Gates. Very thankful for your efficient aid to our expeditions. BARTON.

Harpoot, June 6, 1896.

BARTON, Constantinople.

Your agents now meeting no difficulties whatever. Am most happy to assist your wonderfully successful work.

FONTANA.

Palou, June 6, 1896.

BARTON, Constantinople.

Wistar left before your telegram arrived. I will remain. The list of the needy has been made with great care. The recent relief distributed to the poor is as follows; Twelve hundred suits clothing, sixty-five thousand piasters in money, and one thousand pieces bed clothing; seven hundred sets tools have been made by blacksmiths; fifteen thousand persons in district. We will remain here ten days more. One thousand liras is needed in Silouan; the destitution there in proportion is very great.

WOOD.

Marash, June 6, 1896.

BARTON, Constantinople.

Your last remittance, two hundred liras, practically cured the sick, whose number is now small. Have spent nearly all the tool money. People are prayerfully grateful to you. Need of tools, animals and food very pressing. Four thousand liras would enable us to help every family to some extent. Farmers who have implements are working their fields as much as they can without animals. Have written particulars.

MACALLUM.

Constantinople, June 7, 1896.

GATES, American, Harpoot.

The five thousand liras sent you for my men was for work cattle, tools and seed as asked for, and for no other purpose. Please so instruct. Is Wistar coming out now? Kindly send following to Hubbell. Don't know his address.

HUBBELL, American, ————

The five thousand liras sent Gates is all the money there is to finish the field. It is to be used only for work cattle, seed and tools, none for general distribution. Finish your work and return here as near July first as possible. Wood must draw one thousand liras for Diarbekir Vilayet. Please go to Harpoot and take charge of cattle distribution; this is your specialty. This will enable Wood to go to Farkin at once. In that way you can finish together. Answer on receipt of this.

BARTON.

Constantinople, June 8, 1896.

WOOD, American, Palou.

Your telegram received. The money sent was for oxen, tools, and seed, as asked for. Against orders, and dangerous to distribute money. The five thousand liras sent Gates for all expeditions must be divided so as to finish the work there. We have no more funds to send. Draw one thousand liras from the five thousand, to finish your work in Diarbekir. Use it with all expedition and report at Constantinople as near July first as possible.   BARTON.

(We had ordered that no Red Cross cash should be distributed. Wood had been giving out a small amount of missionary money at the special request of Dr. Gates, which we knew nothing of at the time. We heartily approved his course when we learned the facts.)

Arabkir, June 10, 1896.

BARTON, Constantinople.

Wood has received your telegram; he will go to Diarbekir next week. Wistar is in Harpoot. Our dragoman is buying cattle in Arabkir. We return to Harpoot in ten days, afterwards will go to Malatia. Typhus is diminishing from day to day. All well.   HUBBELL.

Constantinople, June 10, 1896.

GATES, American, Harpoot.

Wood's letter just received. Explains money distribution in Palou. Very wise. Exceeding glad he could help you. Feared it was our special seed, tool and cattle fund, already too small. Please send following telegram to Wood:

WOOD, American, ————.

Report of your splendid work just received by mail. We are grateful to you for your heroic efforts. Did not understand about money distribution. It is all right. Keep well.   BARTON.

TELEGRAMS.

Constantinople, June 11, 1896.

HUBBELL, American, Arabkir.

Telegram received. Plans good; all the work excellent; Wood doing grandly. Your dispatch of 16th came late. Porte took official action promptly. Your "notes" here. All well. BARTON.

Constantinople, June 12, 1896.

MACALLUM, American, Marash.

Your dispatch and letter of the situation there, received. Our little balance can only be used for cattle, tools, seed. Draw for fifteen hundred liras—every lira we can possibly spare now. We regret it is beyond our power to send the four thousand desired, for we well know the need there and what excellent work has been done with so little.

BARTON.

Palou, June 19, 1896.

BARTON, Constantinople.

You misunderstood my telegram. The 65,000 piasters was missionary money which could be distributed in no other way. We are distributing in the villages only tools, clothing, bedding, cattle, and grain. Cannot finish distributions here and Diarbekir by July first. Silouan is seven days from here. Your telegram of May 15 is just received. Our work is progressing well. WOOD.

Constantinople, June 20, 1896.

GATES, Harpoot.

Telegraphed you to draw 5,000 liras which we deposited with Peet, June 2. Have you drawn it? Do our men know about the amount? Are they using it? Answer. BARTON.

Constantinople, June 20, 1896.

MACALLUM, American, Marash.

Wired you June 12 to draw fifteen hundred liras for seed, cattle, tools. Have you done so? Answer. BARTON.

Harpoot, June 21, 1896.

BARTON, Constantinople.

Wistar will finish his distribution of cattle and tools next week. Wood started Farkin to-day. Our dragoman still buying cattle. Hintlian with sick in Arabkir. Bush goes Malatia with us next week. Good work, all well.

HUBBELL.

TELEGRAMS.

Harpoot, June 23, 1896.

BARTON, Constantinople.
Your men are using the money and working splendidly.
GATES.

Marash, June 23, 1896.

BARTON, Constantinople.
Money received; many thanks. Macallum left Wednesday for Zeitoun and surrounding villages.
MRS. HENRIETTE MACALLAM.

Constantinople, June 24, 1896.

MACALLUM, American, Marash.
Telegram received. Draw five hundred liras more for cattle, tools, seed.
BARTON.

(Additional sums of money had been received from America since we sent the 5,000 liras to Harpoot, which enabled us to finish the field to better advantage.)

Harpoot, June 27, 1896.

BARTON, Constantinople.
Hubbell's party started for Constantinople to-day. Wistar and Wood go after a week.
FONTANA.

Silouan, June 27, 1896.

BARTON, Constantinople.
Have arrived at Farkin; fourteen hundred sets tools are enroute here from Diarbekir. The Turkish officials are giving us great assistance, and are in no way interfering. Leave for Harpoot in three days.
WOOD.

Harpoot, July 3, 1896.

BARTON, Constantinople.
Wood and I start for Constantinople. Please notify my wife by wire.
WISTAR.

(Dr. Hubbell and men arrived in Constantinople July 16. Mr. Wistar and Mr. Wood on the 20th of same month.)

I need not attempt to say with what gratitude I welcomed back these weary, brown-faced men and officers from a field at once so difficult and so perilous, and none the less did the gratitude of my heart go out to my faithful and capable Secretary Pullman, who had toiled early and late, never leaving for a day, till the face grew thin and the eyes hollow, striving with tender heart that all should go well, and "The children might be fed."

And when the first greetings were over, and the first meal partaken, the full chorus of manly voices: "Home Again," "Sweet Land of Liberty," "Nearer My God to Thee," that rolled out through the open windows of the Red Cross headquarters in Constantinople, fell on the listening ears of Christian and Moslem alike, and though the tones were new and strange all felt that to someone, somewhere, they meant more than mere notes of music.

RED CROSS PRINCIPLES.

Owing to the importance of the subject, it has been decided to place the subjoined statement on a page by itself. rather than embody it in the continuous matter of the report. Evident confusion exists in the minds of our people in regard to the methods of Red Cross relief. We desire to state so emphatically that those who run may read, that THE AMERICAN NATIONAL RED CROSS NEVER APPEALS NOR SOLICITS AID FOR ANY PURPOSE. It does not even adopt the customary and popular practice of raising money by entertainments, as teas, fairs, etc. We are from time to time made aware of the existence of such methods for raising money, apparently by the Red Cross. These are by outside societies or bodies using its unprotected name and insignia for local objects of their own, and to which object they are applied, never finding their way to the relief work of the National organization.

It is a principle which we have always steadfastly maintained that charity and beneficence were degraded by being reduced to a dependence upon a system of beggary. This principle we have not only openly advocated but rigidly carried out in practice.

Some readers may recall an article appearing in the New York *Tribune* of May, 1896, from which we make the following brief extract:

"A moment's reflection will be sufficient to recall to your readers the fact that in all the fourteen years of the existence of the Red Cross in America, and on almost a score of fields where it has administered relief, they have never been appealed to by it for contributions. Its first and strong principles are, never to ask for help. Its method is to go instantly, with its own funds, to a field of reported disaster, simply giving notice of the fact that it goes, investigate, and on learning the situation, faithfully report the same to the people through all public channels, and private sources as well. This information, which can be thoroughly relied upon, has always been held sufficient.

"It takes the ground that the American people, intelligent, humane and liberal, require only to be assured of a real need, and shown an avenue by which it can be reached with relief, to call from them the proper action; they are as humane as ourselves, and need no appeal for generosity from us. The Red Cross will continue to state conditions plainly, but claims no monopoly of charity."

IN MEMORIAM.

It was, perhaps, largely the tender mother love for her son, Ernest, that moved Mrs. Emma Mason, at almost the last day, to accompany us. The family had lived much abroad in Oriental countries, were familiar with several of the languages, and the young son was engaged by us as linguist.

The mother's object was to reach Italy as a favorite residence. She had just recovered from a severe illness in Washington. In London a severe cough attacked her, which increased as time wore on. After a few days of active life in Constantinople, she was reduced to her bed. The best medical skill of the city, both English and Italian was secured. One disease developed another, until it was needful to remove her to the Italian hospital for closer attention than could be given at home. Some of us were with her every day. She remained cheerful and hopeful till the last and left us on the night of the 24th of March.

Every attention was bestowed by the officers of the Legation and Consulate-General, and it was a little official cortege of sympathizing American hearts that followed the peaceful remains, hidden under the lilies and violets of spring, to the beautiful Italian cemetery where they still repose.

"A sweeter spirit ne'er drew breath,
Than my son's wife Elizabeth."

CONTENTS.

	PAGE
EXECUTIVE REPORT—MISS CLARA BARTON	3
COMMENDATORY	38
MARMARA	42
FINANCIAL REPORT—GEORGE H. PULLMAN	45
FINANCIAL BALANCE SHEET	54, 55
MAP OF ASIA MINOR	56
FIRST EXPEDITION REPORT—DR. J. B. HUBBELL	59
SPECIAL MEDICAL REPORT—DR. H. HINTLIAN	73
SECOND EXPEDITION REPORT—EDWARD M. WISTAR	75
THIRD EXPEDITON REPORT—CHARLES KING WOOD	83
FOURTH EXPEDITION REPORT—DR. IRA HARRIS	92
TELEGRAMS	99
RED CROSS PRINCIPLES	120
IN MEMORIAM	122

ILLUSTRATIONS.

Red Cross Headquarters, Constantinople.
                        (Ernest Mason.)

Rev. Joseph K. Greene, D. D., Constantinople.

Ceremony of "Salamlic."

The Outer, or Pera Bridge.

Rev. Henry O. Dwight, D. D.

W. W. Peet, Esq.

Sublime Porte, Stamboul.

View from Red Cross Headquarters.

American Bible House in Stamboul.

Manner of Carrying Burdens, etc.
                        (From Sketches by J. B. Hubbell.)

Marash.
                        (Ernest Mason.)

A Turkish Village.
                        (Ernest Mason.)

Sinnamod, Suburb of Harpoot.
                        (Ernest Mason.)

A Zaptieh. A Wreck. A Khan. Dr. Hubbell and Guard.
                        (Ernest Mason.)

Red Cross Expedition passing through the Valley of Catch Beard.
                        (From Sketch by C. K. Wood.)

Miss Caroline E. Bush.

First Expedition Embarking on Ferryboat.
                        (Ernest Mason.)

Rev. H. N. Barnum, D. D.

Rev. C. F. Gates, D. D.

Interior of Gregorian Church at Oorfa.
                        (From Sketch by C. K. Wood.)

Rev. George Washburn, D. D.

Robert College.

Cistern of the Thousand Columns.

Wall Tower, Diarbekir.

Tools, Agricultural Implements, Weapons, etc.
                      (From Sketches by J. B. Hubbell.)

Red Cross Headquarters, Farkin.
                      (From Sketch by C. K. Wood.)

Harpoot Ruins.
                      (Ernest Mason.)

Section of Red Cross Caravan.

Galata Tower,

Old Tower at Oorfa.

A Bit of Palou.
                      (From Sketch by C. K. Wood.)

Armenian Village of Oulasch.
                      (Ernest Mason.)

Marash.
                      (Ernest Mason.)

Egin.
                      (Ernest Mason.)

Kourdish Mountain Village.
                      (Ernest Mason.)

Turkish Telegram, Original and Translation.

Heading used on Turkish Telegrams.

Distributing Spinning Wheels at Arabkir.
                      (Ernest Mason.)

Aintab.

Constantinople Dogs.

Section of the Outer Wall.

A Coffee House in Pera.

Group of Hammals.

Section of Turkish Cemetery at Scutari.

A Hammal.

Plane Tree of the Janizaries, Stamboul.

www.ingramcontent.com/pod-product-compliance
Lightning Source LLC
Chambersburg PA
CBHW030351170426
43202CB00010B/1343